The Forgotten Ripper

Original Newspaper Accounts of the Thames Torso Murders: 1887-1889

Edited & Compiled by

Patrick J Gallagher

ISBN: 1535284927
ISBN-13: 978-1535284929

For Linda

CONTENTS

Introduction

As far as the British press were concerned, the year 1888 was very much the year of “Jack the Ripper”. The still unidentified killer stalked the ill-lit streets of Whitechapel, brutally slaying five prostitutes between August and November of 1888 before slipping back into the shadows from whence he came.

Over more than a century, amateur sleuths have turned their attention to the case, with the result being a long list of potential suspects, none of whom have ever been definitively identified as the “Ripper”.

But while “Jack” was one of the earliest, and undoubtedly the most famous serial killer, he wasn’t the first to fit the profile. Others, such as the Texas “Servant Girl Annihilator” of 1885, while not called such at the time, had staked their claim to being what would become known as “serial killers” before “Jack” plied his gruesome trade.

In fact, it would appear that even at the time that “Jack the Ripper” was chalking up his bloody tally, *another* serial killer was stalking the streets of London.

Between May 1887 and September 1889, the dismembered remains of four women were found in, or in the vicinity of, the Thames River.

Collected here are the original newspaper accounts of these murders, tracing, in the voices of the time, the events, theories, and pursuit of a “forgotten Ripper”.

While the murders were covered extensively by the press at the time, they did not cause the lasting sensation of the “Ripper” murders, and have largely been forgotten by all but devoted “Jack the Ripper” enthusiasts.

Why?

For one, the murders were spread out over more than two years, compared to the few months it took “Jack” to rack up his body count.

The murders were also spread out a little further geographically, the bodies being found in Rainham, Whitehall, Pimlico and Whitechapel. This last, a brutal murder on the “Ripper’s” turf in September of 1889, led to initial fears that “Jack” had resumed his operations, although due to the *modus operandi* this notion was soon dismissed by the authorities.

Of the four victims, only one was ever identified, due to an initial stroke of luck involving some evidence left with the third body, and good detective work on the part of Scotland Yard. None of the heads of any of the victims were ever recovered, making identification well-nigh impossible without any additional evidence, of which there was very little. The assumption was that the heads were either disposed of more thoroughly to deter identification, or that they were kept as gruesome trophies.

Finally, there were never any real suspects, especially none that could conceivably link to all four victims. While initial leads were chased down in each case, all potential suspects were eventually cleared. There is almost nothing for the modern amateur sleuth to go in comparison to the laundry list of suspects in the “Ripper” murders.

But for all that, the case is an intriguing one. There can be no doubt that the killer deliberately toyed with the police in the way he disposed of the body parts, in some cases quite publicly. In the case of the second murder, the culprit left the torso of the victim in the basement of a construction site in Whitehall, just a few blocks from the Houses of Parliament. The building under construction on the site was nothing less than the new headquarters for Scotland Yard.

The number of leads are few, the number of theories just as thin on the ground. But the case of the "Thames Torso Murderer", this "Forgotten Ripper", is one which holds just as much mystery, if not more, as his more famous counterpart.

CASE 1

The Rainham Torso

May 1887

Morning Post - Friday 13 May 1887

A Thames Mystery.

On Wednesday morning the lower portion of the trunk of a female was washed ashore on the bank of the Thames at Rainham, Essex. The remains were taken charge of by the police, and Dr. Calloway, of Barking, pronounced the remains to be those of a young woman of 28 to 30 years of age. The severing of the bones had been accomplished by means of a very fine instrument, and the flesh was cut as if by a person skilled in surgical operations. No other portions of the body were found, and there were no means of ascertaining when the body was dissected, but the opinion is that it must have been within a very recent period. Superintendent Dobson, of Brentwood, is making inquiries in the matter. An inquest will be held at Rainham, and meanwhile the river bank is being searched for the missing portions of the body.

Gloucestershire Echo - Friday 13 May 1887

Portions the body of a young woman have been washed ashore on the banks of the Thames at Rainham. Some of the limbs had been dismembered as if with a sharp instrument, and by one skilled in surgery.

Chelmsford Chronicle - Friday 13 May 1887

HORRIBLE DISCOVERY AT RAINHAM.
SUPPOSED MURDER.
A MUTILATED BODY FOUND IN THE RIVER.

No little excitement was created at Rainham on Wednesday, when it became known that a bargeman named Hughes had found floating in the river, near Rainham Ferry, a portion of the body of a woman. The legs, arms, shoulders, and head were missing, and there is not much doubt as to its being a case of murder. The remains were tied up a piece of canvas. The body has been examined by medical gentlemen, who believe it to be that of a woman of from 24 to 26 years of age. It had been in the water about a fortnight.

An inquest will be held by Mr. C. C. Lewis at the Phoenix Hotel to-morrow (Saturday).

Lancashire Evening Post - Saturday 14 May 1887

MYSTERIOUS DISCOVERY IN ESSEX. HORRIBLE MUTILATION OF A BODY.

Yesterday morning the officers of the Criminal Investigation Department were busily engaged making inquiries with respect to a mysterious discovery at Rainham Ferry, Rainham, Essex, of the trunk of a young woman. The trunk was found in the water by some workmen, it being wrapped in some rough canvas. On the trunk being examined by the police surgeon it was found to have belonged to a woman of about 28 or 29 years old. The hip bones had been taken out of the sockets, and the body otherwise more or less mutilated. The manner in which this had been done showed clear evidence that the person or persons who did it had a knowledge of dissection. The appearance of the trunk indicated that it must have been in the water between two and three weeks. The top part of the trunk, and the head, arms, and legs being missing, the police have been searching for the remainder. On the canvas in which the trunk was wrapped no marks or names were found, or anything which can lead to the identity of the original owner. An inquest will be held.

Shields Daily Gazette - Saturday 14 May 1887

THE RAINHAM MYSTERY.

An inquest was opened at Rainham, Essex, to-day, upon the remains of a female which were found in the Thames on Wednesday. The discovery had caused much local excitement, as the remains had been enclosed in a bag, after being cut to pieces. Evidence was first taken as to the discovery of the bag by a lighterman, it having been washed ashore by the tide at Rainham Ferry. A constable deposed that the knot on the bag was an ordinary one and not a sailor's Knot. Medical testimony was to the effect that the trunk had been sawn through by a fine sharp saw. There was neither head nor legs in the bag. The cuts in the rest of the remains had evidently been done by some one expert in the use of the knife. The doctor further testified that the remains look as if some one had attempted to get rid of the body piecemeal. The person who cut it up was evidently thoroughly acquainted with anatomy. The inquest was then adjourned.

Sheffield Daily Telegraph - Monday 16 May 1887

THE RIVER MYSTERY. MURDER OR MEDICAL STUDENTS' MISCHIEF?

An inquest held at Rainham, near Chelmsford, Saturday on the body of a woman which was found tied up in a bag at Rainham Ferry on Wednesday without the slightest mark of identification. Dr. Callaway stated that the body, which was that of a woman of about 27, had been cut in pieces by an expert. It looked as though someone had attempted to get rid the body piecemeal. He was quite sure, however, that a very skilful person, one acquainted with anatomy, had cut it up. Superintendent Dobson, the Essex County Constabulary, expressed the opinion that the body had not been taken from a dissecting-room; the hospitals being very careful and particular, and he had no idea that this was part of a dissected body. The inquiry was then adjourned for three weeks.

Yorkshire Post and Leeds Intelligencer - Friday 20 May 1887

THE GHASTLY DISCOVERY AT RAINHAM.

No further portions of the body of the woman supposed to have been murdered, whose trunk was discovered in the Thames at Rainham, Essex, have been found up to the present, but the police feel sanguine that the search among the various creeks and bights of the river will ultimately prove successful, and the recovery of the head in particular is looked forward to as a complete means of establishing identification. In all probability the part of the body already found will be placed in methylated spirit, with the view of preservation, so that when the other portions come to light they can be fitted together, as in the case of Harriet Lane, the victim of the Wainwright murder. It is anticipated that a reward will be offered as an inducement to the riverside men to keep their eyes open. The medical aspect of the case is entirely opposed to the idea that the case is one of dissection, for although the body has been most carefully and scientifically dismembered, the elements of dissection, as practised in the hospitals, are entirely wanting. Moreover, no body of a woman, such the one described, is missing from any dissecting-room, and the Scotland Yard authorities are entirely in accord with Dr. Calloway in attributing the death of the woman to foul play. The deceased is supposed to be woman of 27 or 29, dark, well formed and well nourished, and that her death took place about May 2d or 3d. Any information should be sent to Superintendent Shore of Scotland Yard, Whitehall, S.W.

Chelmsford Chronicle - Friday 20 May 1887

A CRIME, OR A GHASTLY HOAX?

Various conjectures are rife with regard to the horrible discovery made at Rainham last week, but at present there appears to be little chance of the mystery becoming elucidated. The finding of the body of a woman, minus head, legs, and arms, would naturally suggest a most shocking murder, but there are circumstances which throw some doubt on this supposition. The clean manner in which the limbs were removed has given rise to the belief that the body had been thrown into the river by medical students after dissection, but at the inquest Mr. Lewis (the coroner), Dr. Calloway, and Supt. Dobson did not think this solution of the mystery was the correct one. It was pointed out that a register is kept of the way in which every dissected body is disposed of, and, moreover, the disposal of a body in this way would be a contravention of the Anatomical Act. If a murder has been committed it would appear to be one of the most atrocious ever perpetrated, and, unfortunately, there is at present every prospect of its being added to the long list of unpunished crimes. For the credit of Essex, it should be pointed out that there is no indication of its being an Essex crime. The murder, if murder it be, was probably committed in London, and the body thrown into the Thames. Another hypothesis is that the body was cast from a passing ship. The discovery would have exactly suited Edgar Allen Poe as the foundation on which to build one of his gruesome and blood-chilling tales.

Chelmsford Chronicle - Friday 20 May 1887

HORRIBLE DISCOVERY AT RAINHAM.
SUPPOSED MURDER.
A MUTILATED BODY FOUND IN THE RIVER.

On Wednesday week the mutilated body of a woman was found in the river Thames by a lighterman named Edward Hughes, under the circumstances detailed in our last issue. The head, arms, and legs are missing.

A later account says:- "The severing of the bones had been accomplished by means of a very fine instrument, and the flesh was cut as if by a person skilled in surgical operations. No other portions of the body were found, and there were no means of ascertaining when the body was dissected, but the opinion is that it must have been within a very recent period. Superintendent Dobson, of Brentwood, is making inquiries in the matter. The river bank is being searched for the missing portions of the body."

THE INQUEST

Mr. C. C. Lewis, coroner, held an inquest on the body at the Phoenix Hotel, on Saturday morning. Mr. F. S. Hempleman was foreman of the jury.

Edward Hughes, a licensed lighterman, of Victoria Docks, said that about 11.30 on Wednesday morning he was on his barge at Rainham Ferry; the barge was lying alongside the jetty at Mr. Hempleman's factory; the tide was flowing; he saw what appeared to be a bag, which the tide was washing up; the bag was about 30 feet from his barge; he went to it and brought it to shore; as he was picking the bag up it partially came undone, and he saw it contained part of the body of a woman; he told a man who was coming up into Rainham to inform the police; he left the body on the shore in charge of another lighterman; he did not see any papers or any linen in the bag; he saw nothing but the body of the woman.

P.C. Stock, stationed at Rainham, deposed that about 12.30 on Wednesday morning he received information which induced him to proceed to Rainham Ferry; on the shore near Mr. Hempleman's factory he found a piece of sacking, tied up with cord; it was partially undone, and he could see it was part of the body of a woman; it was at once taken to a shed at the Ferry public-house, and then removed to the Phoenix Hotel; Dr. Calloway saw it the next day; it presented about the same appearance as it did when found; he was present when the sack was undone altogether.

The Coroner: Was there any linen or paper in the sack which would throw any light on the case? – Witness: No, sir.

And you have not heard anything since? – No, sir.

A Juror: Did you notice whether there were any letters or any mark of any kind on the sacking? - No, sir.

Was there anything peculiar in the cord with which the sack was tied? – No.

Dr. Calloway said that on Thursday he was shown part of the body of a female; it consisted of the trunk of the body, with two and a half bones of the vertebrae above the trunk; the legs had been sawn through completely straight with a fine sharp saw; the integuments round the spine were also cut through by a clean sharp instrument; the head, legs, and arms were missing; the thighs had been taken clean out from the sockets of the pelvis, the muscles at the side being cut obliquely from the inside to the outside; these were also clean cuts and must have been done by a sharp instrument; with all the incisions there was no jaggedness, and they appeared to have been done by an expert; he could not detect any violence to the body; it appeared to have been dead about a fortnight, although it might not have been in the water quite so long; he should think the body was that of a woman from 27 to 29; it was well nourished.

The Coroner: With reference to the dissecting rooms, it would be contrary to the Anatomical Act to allow a body to be taken away.

Witness: Oh yes. Continuing, Dr. Callloway said it seemed to him that somebody wished to get rid of the body by piecemeal; it must have been done by a skilled person.

The Coroner: Your opinion is that the body has been cut in the way you suggest for the purpose of lessening the bulk? – Witness: Yes.

Mr. Hempleman: There were no marks or moles or anything of that sort that could possibly lead to identification? – Witness: No.

Supt. Dobson, of Brentwood, said he went to Rainham on Wednesday in company with Inspector Allen, and saw the body; he examined the body on Thursday with Dr. Calloway, but found no marks by which it could be identified; the same afternoon he went to Scotland-yard and saw the head of the department, to whom he gave all particulars; there was no record of anyone missing; the information was at once circulated throughout the Metropolitan police district.

A Juryman (to Dr. Calloway): You don't think this body could have been taken from a dissecting room?

D. Calloway: No.

Supt. Dobson: I made enquiries at Scotland-yard, and Supt. Shaw told me they were very particular about the bodies; I knew that myself.

The Coroner: There is no doubt about that. There is a complete account kept of the bodies that are dissected.

The Foreman: And how are they disposed of?

Dr. Calloway: Oh, yes. There is a register kept of every body which is dissected.

The Coroner said the only course the jury could adopt was to adjourn the inquiry to a distant date to give a chance of other portions of the body being found if they had been got rid of in the same way. Of course they might have been taken in another direction altogether. But if the other portions were done up in similar parcels and deposited anywhere on the Thames it was possible they might be found. Through the press the particulars would be ventilated and watermen and others would be on the look out.

The inquiry was then adjourned until June 3rd.

THE SEARCH FOR FURTHER REMAINS.

During the whole of Saturday and Sunday the Scotland-yard authorities and the county police were engaged in an attempt to solve the mystery, and to find the missing portions of the body, but without success. Assuming that the whole body, but in different bundles, was consigned to the river at the same time, it was thought possible that the tide might have washed a further package into some of the creeks and bays which abound throughout the Essex coast, and as a large quantity of wreckage is washed up into a small bight close by the spot where the first bundle was discovered, this was searched first, though without success. Shore men, who know every inch of the river's bank, are tolerably sanguine that the search will prove successful, and boats are out in all directions.

Up to Tuesday no further portion of the body had been found. In all probability the part of the body already found will be placed in methylated spirit, with a view o preservation, so that when the other portions come to light they can be fitted together, as in the case of Harriet Lane, the victim of the Wainwright murder. It is anticipated that a reward will be offered as an inducement to the riverside men to keep their eyes open. The medical aspect of the case is entirely opposed to the idea that the case is one of dissection, for although the body has been most carefully and scientifically dismembered, the elements of dissection, as practiced in the hospitals, are entirely wanting. Moreover, no body of a woman such as the one described is missing from any dissecting room, and the Scotland-yard authorities are entirely in accord with Dr. Calloway in attributing the death of the woman to foul play.

Illustrated Police News - Saturday 28 May 1887

HORRIBLE DISCOVERY OF HUMAN REMAINS AT RAINHAM.

Lancashire Evening Post - Friday 03 June 1887

THE HORRIBLE DISCOVERY AT RAINHAM

The inquest on the body of an unknown woman, part of whose trunk was found in the Thames on the 11th ult., was resumed at Rainham, Essex, to-day. The postmortem examination proved that the deceased met her death by foul means, and that the limbs had been severed by a skilled person. The police had been unable to find friends, and, although diligent search had been made, the missing portions of the body could not be found. An open verdict was returned, the jury leaving matters with the police.

Reynolds's Newspaper - Sunday 05 June 1887

THE RAINHAM MYSTERY.

Mr. C.C. Lewis resumed, at the Phoenix tavern, Rainham, on Friday, the adjourned inquiry relative to the death of a female unknown, part of whose body was discovered in the Thames on the 11th ult.

At the opening of the inquiry three weeks ago evidence was given that on the morning of the 11th ult., a lighterman named Edwards discovered a parcel floating in the Thames off Rainham, and upon opening it found that it contained the lower half of the body of a female.

On Friday, Dr. Calloway was recalled, and said there was nothing on the body which would give the slightest indication as to the manner in which the deceased came by her death. All he could say was that the body had been dismembered very shortly after death.

Mr. Dobson, the superintendent of the Essex county constabulary, recalled, stated that since the adjournment of the inquest every inquiry had been made with the view of ascertaining the name and antecedents of the deceased woman, and special inquiries and researches had been undertaken in the hope of discovering some further portions of the murdered woman's body; but without the least success. He had received a letter from a Mrs. Cross, of Albanyterrace, Marsh-gate, Richmond, Surrey, giving information of the loss of her daughter, who had disappeared from her home. The description of that person tallied exactly with the supposed appearance of the dead woman. The young woman (Miss Cross) was of weak intellect, and would absent herself from home for several days. She would wander to the side of the river, and get upon any barge or boats which might happen to be moored alongside the towing path. This occurred frequently, but before the date of the supposed murder Miss Cross disappeared, and had never since been heard of.

The Coroner, in summing up, said the deceased had, no doubt, been the victim of foul play; but nothing leading to a clue to the incriminated parties had been discovered.

The jury returned an open verdict.

Gloucestershire Echo - Monday 06 June 1887

Another parcel, containing further portions of the mutilated remains of a woman, concerning whose death an inquest was held last week at Rainham, was found the Thames on Sunday, near the Victoria Embankment. It is thought other portions the body will be washed up in few days.

St James's Gazette - Monday 06 June 1887

THE RAINHAM MYSTERY.
ANOTHER DISCOVERY.

A pierman at the Temple observed yesterday a parcel floating near the pier, and having secured it, found that it contained a human thigh, wrapped up in a piece of coarse canvas and tied with a piece of cord corresponding with that round the package found in the Thames off Rainham Ferry some weeks ago, which enclosed the upper portion of the body of young woman.

Pall Mall Gazette - Tuesday 07 June 1887

Yet another Thames mystery! And if the opinion of the experts is to be depended on, a mystery and a murder of the most diabolical kind. On the 11th of May, the trunk of a human body was found off Rainham, in Essex, wrapped in coarse sacking and sewed with thick cord. Where were the missing limbs? Gone out to sea with the sewage and nameless flotsam and jetsam? The experts thought not. They said the rest of the body was in the dissecting room, and laughed at the horrible joke of some reckless medical students. Now they have formed a different opinion. On Sunday a discoloured and swollen thigh was washed up against the Temple Stairs. The thigh of Sunday fitted in with the trunk of the 11th of May. The covering of the parcel newly found is of the same description as the wrapping of the other part of the body; the same minute surgical and anatomical knowledge is shown in the dissection of both parts. And the coroners say it is "murder." At the same time a Mrs. Cross, of Richmond, comes forward and tells a strange story of a daughter missing since January. The police have certainly not much of a clue to work upon.

Sheffield Evening Telegraph - Tuesday 07 June 1887

CLUE TO THE RAINHAM MYSTERY.

With regard to the discovery of portions of the mutilated remains of a young woman in the Thames near Rainham Ferry last month, and the further discovery of another part of what is believed to be the same body near the Temple Pier on Sunday, a correspondent yesterday had an interview with the Mrs. Cross, of Richmond, whose daughter has been missing from home for some time. Mrs. Cross stated that her daughter was somewhat strange in her mind at times, and had an impediment in her speech. She was in the habit of going to the ferry at Richmond, where barges, &c, were moored, but always returned home until the last occasion, when she disappeared at seven o'clock on the morning of January 20. Since that time, however, nothing whatever had been heard of her, although the police were at once notified of the disappearance, and her description circulated. The latter was as follows:- Age 28, height 5ft. 8in., complexion dark, eyes dark, pencilled eyebrows, short curly black hair, and exceedingly handsome face. Mrs. Cross stated that shortly before she missed her daughter the latter went out one evening shopping, and was accosted by a strange man, who said that he could show her the nearest way home. She walked with him some distance, when he suddenly demanded her parcels and money, stating that if she did not give them to him he would cut her throat. She gave him all she had, and the man disappeared, but she ran to the Barnes Police Station and gave information. All search, however, for the man was fruitless. - The age and general physical development of Miss Cross, with that of the murdered woman, are considered by competent authorities to be identical.

Morning Post - Wednesday 08 June 1887

The Rainham Mystery.

Yesterday morning the police were engaged in an endeavour to ascertain whether the two pieces of the body found in the Thames were those of Miss Cross, who mysteriously disappeared from her mother's house at Richmond, Surrey, a few months ago, and of whom no trace whatever has yet been discovered. There are certain physical peculiarities in the remains found corresponding very closely with the description of Miss Cross, and it is more than possible that the first clue has been obtained. - Yesterday, morning Mr. Langham, the coroner for the city of London, stated that he had received information of the discovery of the thigh, and its removal to the City mortuary in Golden-lane, hut he did not purpose issuing a warrant for the holding of an inquest. In the first place, the thigh was not a body; and, secondly, as there was reason to believe that it belonged to the half trunk found at Rainham, upon which an inquest had already been opened, he considered that it should be sent on to the same place.

Lloyd's Weekly Newspaper - Sunday 12 June 1887

THE RAINHAM MURDER MYSTERY. DISCOVERY OF FURTHER REMAINS.

On Sunday the thigh of a woman was found in the Thames off the Temple stairs, which is supposed to be part of the body of which the lower half of the trunk was found on the 11th of last month, off Rainhain in Essex. The limb was removed to the City mortuary.

On Wednesday evening, on the foreshore of Battersea pier, was found a piece of coarse canvas tied with a string. On being opened it was found to contain the thorax of a human body, supposed to be that of a woman, with the lungs and most of the dorsal vertebrae, which later on, being examined by the police-surgeons, were found to have been divided with a sharp instrument.

No trace has been found of the daughter of Mrs. Cross, of Richmond, who disappeared on Jan. 20.

A GRAVE SCANDAL.

Yesterday afternoon Dr. Calloway, of Rainham, had a consultation at Battersea with Mr. A. Braxton Hicks (the district coroner), Dr. Kempster (divisional surgeon), and Inspectors Shore and Eyre (of Scotland-yard), with reference to the portion of a body found at Battersea. -

Previous to the consultation Dr. Calloway, who, it may be remembered, gave evidence at the inquest at Rainham, made careful examination of the remains, and was satisfied that they formed part of the body to which the pelvis which was recently found on the Essex shore belonged, and his theory that the dissection was performed by a man well versed in medical science was more than strengthened. The piece of sacking round the trunk was exactly similar to that found at Rainham, and off the Temple stairs. With regard to the portions of the body found at the last-mentioned place, certain facts have transpired which amount to little short of a scandal. It is stated on good authority that when an inspector from Scotland-yard went to the City mortuary and asked what was going to be done with the thigh, the coroner's officer informed him that he did not know; but, upon being further questioned, he is said to have admitted that the limb had been put into a pauper's coffin and sent to the City of London cemetery at Ilford for burial, although he was not quite certain whether it had been buried. Of course, this was after Mr. Langham had declined to hold an inquest. As a result of yesterday's consultation Mr. A. Braxton Hicks decided not to hold an inquest at present; but he gave Mr. Saxby, his officer, instructions to procure a glass jar and place the remains in spirits of wine. This was done in the course of the afternoon, and the vessel hermetically sealed. The present case strongly points to the necessity for a central mortuary for London, in which bodies or portions of bodies could be preserved for some time. Some reform will also be necessary in respect to coroners' courts, which are falling into grave disrepute in many quarters.

Manchester Courier and Lancashire General Advertiser - Saturday 18 June 1887

THE RAINHAM MYSTERY.
REPORTED DISCOVERY OF THE HEAD.

On Tuesday morning it was reported to the police authorities at Barking that the head of the woman supposed to have been murdered on or about the 1st of May last had been recovered. The police there, on being questioned, were unable to say if there was any truth in the statement. Certainly the discovery had not been made in their district. All the attempts of the police to discover if any young woman is missing who would answer to the supposed description of the deceased have at present been without avail, beyond the discovery of the absence of Miss Cross, of Richmond. The parts of the body by which Miss Cross could be identified are, curiously enough, still missing.

Sheffield Independent - Friday 01 July 1887

THE RAINHAM MYSTERY.
AN EXTRAORDINARY STORY.

Yesterday a further discovery of human remains was made at Rainham, a parcel, similar in appearance to the three found respectively at Rainham, Waterloo Bridge, and Battersea, being recovered from the Thames, a short distance from the spot where the original discovery took place. This is looked upon as a very important clue, and it is now believed that it is probable the whole of the body was committed to the water at one time, but in separate parcels. A most extraordinary circumstance yesterday came to light in reference to the murder. A lady has been making inquiries for some time past in regard to the where-abouts of her sister, who she believes has been murdered. She has made a statement to the following effect: - She said that for some time during last year her sister had been keeping company with a young doctor, and she knew that the latter had seduced her, and was actually living upon the proceeds of her industry. Both parties lived in South London, but last year the doctor obtained possession of a practice in a Northern suburb, and went to live there, being followed shortly afterwards by the young woman, who insisted, much against his will, in living with him. They led the neighbours to believe that she was his housekeeper, but she suddenly disappeared about two months ago, and has not since been heard of. Her age and general description answer that of the body found in the Thames, and inquiries are being made with the view of ascertaining whether the young woman is still alive. From inquiries instituted there seems to be some grounds for believing that several “scenes” had taken place between the doctor and his housekeeper, and that she had threatened to expose him if he did not marry her.

St James's Gazette - Saturday 02 July 1887

THE DISCOVERY OF HUMAN REMAINS.

A surgical examination was made at the St. Pancras mortuary yesterday of the limbs found on Thursday in the Regent's Canal. It is said that the indications are such as to lead to the conclusion that they belonged to the body of a woman whose age was probably between twenty and thirty. It is also stated that the canvas in which they were wrapped is of the same kind at that in which portions of a female body were found off Rainham Creek and at Waterloo and Battersea Bridges.

Birmingham Daily Post - Monday 04 July 1887

THE STARTLING DISCOVERIES OF HUMAN REMAINS.

On Saturday morning, upon enquiries being made with respect to the discovery of human remains in the waters of the Regent's Canal at Camden Town, on Thursday and Friday, it was ascertained that the police have not been able to find anything else. The sacking in which the limbs were found having been taken charge of by the officers of the Criminal Investigation Department, it was, upon an examination being made, found to be sacking of the same kind as that which contained the trunk and other portions of a body that was found in the waters of the River Thames, off Rainham Creek, and Waterloo and Battersea Bridges. That being so, the belief that the limbs found in the Camden Town district belonged to the trunk, &c., found in the Thames has become so much strengthened that special instructions were issued from Scotland yard that upon no account were the limbs that are now lying in the mortuary at St. Pancras to be interfered with except on an order from the coroner or from the Home Secretary, and that it was their intention to have a special examination of the limbs made by Dr. Galloway, who examined the trunk minutely at Rainham, with a view to ascertain whether the fragments were identical with the trunk and other portions that he has already seen. If they are almost identical, then the authorities intend to apply to the Home Secretary for an order authorising the exhumation of the trunk and other portions of the body which have been buried, and getting them placed together, with the view, if possible, of obtaining information to lead to the identification of the same, and having an enquiry. The examination already made by several medical men shows that they are the limbs of a well-developed young woman, and a measurement of the legs and feet have been made. The left leg has the kneecap with it, whilst the right has not. The toenails and the skin of the heels have disappeared, laying bare the bones. Around the upper part of the calf of each leg there is a deep mark, but whether these marks were produced before death or since remains for a closer examination to clear up. The police authorities have no doubt that if the medical men agree that the limbs are those that belong to the trunk found in the Thames at Rainham, they will soon be able to clear the case up. A special look-out is being kept by lock-keepers and bargemen on the Regent's Canal, for the purpose, if possible, of finding the missing head and other parts of the body.

Exeter and Plymouth Gazette - Wednesday 06 July 1887

THE DISCOVERY OF HUMAN REMAINS.

The statement published to the effect that a gentleman had made an important communication to a West-end coroner's officer in regard to the recent discoveries of human remains at Rainham and in the Regent's Canal, proves, says a correspondent, to be accurate. The gentleman in question has again waited on the coroner's officer for Westminster, to whom he gave a full description of the supposed missing person. He said:- "It is quite true that on the afternoon of the 17th of last month I saw a woman standing on the pavement near Charing Cross Railway Station, with a loose canvas bag or wrapper in her arms, from which the smell of decomposed human flesh emanated strongly. The idea of a woman standing on the pavement in the Strand, with a portion of a murdered corpse under her arm is not one which would obtain immediate credence with business people. That is just the reason I believe why it actually took place in this instance, and the woman was permitted to go unmolested on her hideous errand. She looked as if she had calculated in this way. I regret that I did not watch her closer than I did, but I can identify her, and surely she ought not to be difficult to find. She had doubtless come to London by the London, Chatham, and Dover Railway to Charing Cross, and was going North, because she had moved some 50 yards eastwards of the station. Her height is about 5ft. 5in., age 48, hair thin and dark, regular features, general contour sharp and slightly elongated, complexion pale, suggesting an indoor life. She was dressed in a bonnet trimmed with some velvet stuff, and a shawl, her entire costume being brown and shabby, though not much worn.

Lloyd's Weekly Newspaper - Sunday 10 July 1887

THE RAINHAM MYSTERY.

About two o'clock on Thursday afternoon some little boys, while fishing in the Regent's canal, near to St. Pancras Lock, situated near the railway goods yard, saw something floating in the water, which, upon closer examination, proved to be part of a human being. They informed a man named Henley, who accompanied them back to the water's edge, and with the aid of one of the fishing- rods brought the parcel to shore and conveyed it to St. Pancras mortuary. Dr. McFarlane, assistant divisional surgeon, proceeded to the mortuary, and on examination pronounced it to be the leg of a young woman. At 7.35 p.m., Police-constable Robert Aitken was on duty in the Albert-road, Regent's-park, midway between Gloucester gate and St. Mark's bridges, when his attention was called to some boys on the towing-path of the canal, who seemed in an excited state, and were endeavouring to get something on shore. Thinking it was some one drowning, he jumped over the two sets of palings, and on reaching the towing-path he discovered that the object which had attracted the observation of the boys was a parcel containing another human leg. He removed it to the Albany-street police-station. The legs were each wrapped in canvas and tied with cord. The legs are believed to form part of the body of a female well developed, aged from 25 to 30. The feet are small and well formed, and the contour of the ankles and calves is such as one would expect to find in a person of decent birth. One most important point which may lead to identification is the fact that in the front of both legs are evidences of some kind of congestion, such as varicose veins or other similar appearances.

It is conjectured that the portions of the body found in the Regent's canal are those missing from the corpse discovered at Rainham, and efforts are now being made to ascertain with some degree of certainty whether all the portions do or do not belong to the same body. It will be recollected that the first piece found on the 11th of last May was the lower half of the bust of a well-developed woman of 27 or thereabouts; that the lower viscera had been carefully extracted, and that the thighs had been taken from their sockets. A fortnight afterwards a thigh minus the leg was found, and five days after that the lungs, thorax, and upper part of the dorsal vertebrae were recovered from the Thames at Battersea. The appearances of these fragments were almost identical, as regards age, development, and date of death. There are no traces of hospital dissection or operative surgery, the only two phases of surgical science now resorted to in post-mortem cases. If the theory that the legs and feet now found belong to the Rainham trunk, the body is not that of Miss Cross, of Richmond, as her parents state that her feet were abnormally large whereas in the present case those extremities are remarkably small.

Shields Daily Gazette - Tuesday 12 July 1887

THE LONDON MYSTERY.

An inquest on the portions of human remains lately discovered in the Regent's Canal was opened yesterday afternoon by the Middlesex coroner. The police and other witnesses having proved finding the limbs of a female in different parts of the canal, Inspector Hare proved finding the lower part of the trunk at Rainham. Dr. Galloway, of Barking, stated his opinion that the portions belonged to the same body. The inquiry was adjourned for a month, as the Home Secretary is making special inquiries in the matter.

Chelmsford Chronicle - Friday 15 July 1887

The Mysterious Discovery of Human Remains.

On Monday Dr. G. Danford Thomas held an inquest at the Crowndale Hall, Camden Town, concerning the discovery of two arms and legs in the Regent's Canal . - The Coroner said it was supposed that a body had been cut up by some scientific man, but it was possible that the case was one of murder. Evidence of the finding of the legs and arms having been given, Detective-Inspector Arthur Hare, of Scotland-yard, said that on May 11th the lower portion of a female's trunk was discovered at Rainham Ferry. Upon this an inquest was held by Mr. Lewis, and at that inquiry an open verdict was returned. On June 5 in the Thames a thigh was found off Temple Pier. The limb was buried, but it was now intended to exhume it. On June 8 the chest of a woman was found at Battersea, with the breasts cut off. - Dr. Edwin Calloway, of Barking, stated that he examined the trunk that was found at Rainham, and it was that of a female, about 26 years of age. The thigh found in the Thames corresponded with the trunk. The chest also corresponded exactly with the trunk, and had been sawn through. The collarbone and the breasts had been taken off. He formed the opinion that the trunk had been in the water about a fortnight, and it was his opinion that the death of the woman took place in May. He also saw the remains found in St. Pancras, and he was of opinion that they belonged to the same body. The canvas in which they were found was similar to that in which the other parts except that of the thigh were found. He was of opinion that the body had been cut up by a person having a knowledge of the human body. - The Coroner said it was a very grave matter indeed, and it was advisable that it should be further gone into, more especially as the Home Secretary had ordered further surgical examination of the remains to be made. - The inquiry was then adjourned till August 6.

Exeter and Plymouth Gazette - Monday 18 July 1887

ANOTHER REGENT'S CANAL MYSTERY.

On Saturday evening the Metropolitan Police received a parcel which had just been found in the Regent's Canal at Camden Town, and which contained the left thigh of a woman. It was at first thought that this was an additional portion of the remains of the body discovered at Rainham; but upon examination it was found not to be so, this being evidently the thigh of a woman advanced in years. In the opinion of the surgeon it had been in the water about six weeks. No further portion the body had been recovered up to last night, but a strict watch is being kept.

Sheffield Daily Telegraph - Thursday 21 July 1887

A GRIM INCIDENT IN THE RAINHAM MYSTERY.

The various human remains which have been found from time to time at Rainham, Essex, in the Thames off Waterloo Pier, on the foreshore of the river off Battersea Pier, in the Regent's Canal, Kentish Town, remains comprising the arms (divided), the lower part of the thorax, the pelvis, both thighs, and the legs and feet; in fact, the entire body excepting the head and the upper part of the chest, have all been recovered, and are now in the possession of the police authorities. The portions of the body which were interred at Ilford have been exhumed, but were in a state of decomposition, and these, together with the other portions, have been placed in spirits, after having been proved to belong to one human frame. The remains have been examined by an anatomical expert, who has made an official report, which shows that all the portions of the body are those of a stout, well-nourished female, probably between 25 and 35 years of age. The deceased would probably have dark hair, would probably be about 5 feet 3 inches or 5 feet 4 inches in height, and the time of death would probably be about three months ago. The body had been divided by some one who knew the structure of the human frame, but was not necessarily a skilled anatomist. There are no marks on the portions of the body recovered to show the cause of death or to afford means of identification.

The police authorities state that they will be glad to receive information regarding missing females about this time who may in any way correspond with the particulars ascertained. Information should be given at the nearest police station or at Scotland Yard.

Morning Post - Saturday 30 July 1887

FICTITIOUS NEWS.

James Greville Burns attended at the Mansion House Police-court yesterday on an adjourned summons charging him with having obtained 23s. by false pretences from the cashier of the *Evening News*. - The alleged fraud was in connection with certain reports furnished by the defendant in relation to what was headed “The Regent’s Canal and Rainham Mysteries.” The defendant represented that a gentleman of unimpeachable veracity had communicated to Mr. Ralph, the coroner’s officer, at Westminster, information of having seen a woman with a canvas bag which apparently contained a dead body, and that the information had been accepted by the Criminal Investigation Department as a likely clue to the discovery of the criminals. - Mr. Nash, cashier of the paper, proved that after the first and second statements supplied by the defendant, he spoke to him, and the defendant said every word he had written he could prove and vouch for. He also said he had the story from the coroner's officer. The third payment was made to him with the distinct warning that inquiries would be instituted. The defendant persisted that he had received the information from Ralph. - Tom Ralph, police-constable A 839, the coroner's officer for Westminster, said he did not give the defendant any of the information contained in the accounts which appeared. The information was given by the defendant to him, and not by him to the defendant. - This was the case for the prosecution. - Mr. Black, for the defence, urged that there was no false pretence. The defendant never disguised the fact that he himself was the person of veracity who witnessed the occurrence, and he was reporting what he himself saw, and not what others had seen. - Mr. Alderman Evans said the money was obtained on the statement that the information was derived from the coroner's officer, which was untrue. He committed the defendant for trial, but admitted him to bail.

Chelmsford Chronicle - Friday 05 August 1887

Following our remarks last week as to the want of veracity shown by evening papers generally, comes a revelation of the way in which manufactured reports get into print. An enterprising journalist, who appears to add to his legitimate earnings by the fruits of his imagination, was charged at one of the London police-courts with having obtained 23s. by false pretences from the cashier of the *Evening News*. It is alleged that the defendant supplied fictitious reports with reference to the Rainham mystery, and on his insisting that he could vouch for every word he had written, three statements were received, paid for, and published. The statements have all been widely circulated through the London and provincial papers. Certainly a case surrounded by such gruesome features as the Rainham mystery affords a large scope for the efforts of penny-a-liners, and the wordy paragraphs which appeared in the daily papers for weeks afterwards proved that they made the most of their opportunities. But a line must he drawn somewhere, and when it can be proved that these gentlemen lay their imaginations under tribute for "facts" as well as for embellishment, it is very proper to bring the matter before a court of justice. Mr. Burns has been committed for trial, and if he is found guilty and punished other gentlemen of his class will probably taken warning.

Sheffield Evening Telegraph - Monday 08 August 1887

THE RAINHAM MYSTERY.
WOMAN MURDERED AND CUT UP.

On Saturday afternoon Dr. Danford Thomas resumed the inquiry at the Crowndale Hall, Camden Town, concerning the two arms and legs that were discovered in the waters of the Regent's Canal, near the St. Pancras Lock, portions of the body a woman, who is supposed to have been murdered and afterwards cut up. Other parts of the body have been found in the Thames off Rainham, Waterloo Bridge, and elsewhere. The inquiry had been adjourned for the purpose of enabling the police authorities to make inquiries, with a view of tracing out, if possible, who the deceased was, and also to enable a further search being made with the object of discovering the head and other missing portions of the body. On the case being resumed, the coroner said that since the last time that they were there another thigh had been found, and it was supposed to be connected with the other portions found. - William Cope, labourer, stated that upon Saturday, the 16th of last month, whilst he was at work at the Camden Town Locks, he noticed in the Waters of the Regent's Canal, between two barges, a piece of flesh, which on getting out he found was a left thigh, on which he called a police-constable, who took it away. - Detective-inspector Arthur Hare stated that since the adjournment every inquiry with respect to the case had been made, but up to the present no clue to lead to the identity of the woman had been obtained. - Mr. Thomas Bond, F.R.C.S., one the surgeons of the Westminster Hospital, stated that he had examined the different parts recovered, and he found that the whole them corresponded, and were certainly that of the same body. He searched the body, but could not find any marks likely to lead to identification. From a measurement of the different parts he was of opinion that the female was 5ft. 2in, to 5ft. 4in. in height. He concluded that the woman was from 25 to 35 years. From his examination he was of opinion that the woman had never borne a child. The body was that of a well-nourished stout woman, and she had dark hair. The different parts had been divided by some persons having knowledge of anatomy. He was certain that the body had not been divided for dissecting purposes. The parts had been in the water for about three months, and he had no doubt that they were put in at the same time. There was no evidence as to how the deceased came by her death. The head had not been found, and he believed that the weight of the bones would be sufficient to keep it from rising. - The jury returned a verdict "That the remains found were those of a woman between twenty-five and thirty-five years of age, and after hearing the medical evidence they were of opinion that there was not sufficient evidence to show as to how or by what means the said woman came by her death."

CASE 2
The Whitehall Mystery
September 1888

Western Times - Wednesday 12 September 1888

ANOTHER SUPPOSED MURDER AND MUTILATION.

The *Star* in a late edition last night published the following account of a supposed murder and mutilation:- A discovery, which is held to afford incontestable proof of a murder and mutilation, was made in Pimlico to-day (Tuesday). In the canal near Ebury Bridge and Grosvenor-road a policeman's attention was attracted to something which a number of boys were pelting stones at. He had the object of the boys' amusement extricated from the planks of timber amongst which it was entangled, and on examining it found it to be a woman's arm. He had it at once removed to the station; where it was inspected Dr. Neville, of Pimlico-road, the police surgeon. The arm had been removed from the shoulder, and it had evidently been done by an unskilful person. It must have been removed from the body of a person murdered but a day or two, as when touched the blood began to trickle freshly from it. The instrument, too, must have been exceedingly sharp, the joint being cut into and the limb removed at the shoulder socket. There was a cord tied round the arm above the elbow. The person murdered must have been a very fine young woman, as the arm was fully as long as that of a man of five feet ten or five feet eleven. There were a few abrasions on portions of the skin, but these might be caused by knocking against timber in the water. The police deny all knowledge of the subject.

A later telegram says:- A representative of the Press Association had an interview to-night (Tuesday) with Dr Neville, of Pimlico, who examined the arm of the young woman found to-day. He stated that the limb was cut cleanly, but not apparently with a scientific object, so that it is supposed a murder has been committed. The police are making a careful search for other portions of the body.

Hull Daily Mail - Wednesday 12 September 1888

THE PIMLICO MYSTERY.

The Press Association says that although the river in the immediate neighbourhood of the spot where the arm of the young woman was discovered has been dragged, no further portions of the body have been found. The Thames police are assisting in the search. Close to the place where the arm was discovered is a sluice under the embankment wall, from which flows a stream of water from a brewery in the Grosvenor-road.

London Evening Standard - Wednesday 12 September 1888

STRANGE DISCOVERY IN THE THAMES.

About twenty minutes to one yesterday after-noon, Frederick Moore, a man employed at Messrs. Ward's timber yard, Grosvenor-road, had his attention drawn to a curious-looking object, lying on the mud on the bank of the Thames, immediately opposite where he was working. He procured a ladder, and descended to the bank below the wharf. He was startled to find that the object was a human arm. It was fairly wedged between some timber in the wood dock, belonging to Messrs. Chapple. Moore having secured the limb, carefully examined the immediate vicinity, but failing to find any more human remains, he took up the arm, carried it to the embankment, and handed it over to Police-constable Jones, 127 B. Jones wrapped up the arm in paper, and conveyed it to the Gerald-row Police-station. Inspector Adams, of the B Division, after communicating the discovery to Scotland-yard, sent for Dr. Neville, of Pimlico-road and Sloane-street, the nearest medical man, who soon arrived at the police-station, and made a careful examination of the limb. He decided that the arm was that of a well-formed, tall young woman, probably about twenty-five years of age. It had been cut off at the shoulders with some sharp instrument, and the question naturally arose whether this was the work of a professional anatomist or of a murderer. Dr. Neville did not express a positive opinion either way, but said that the work had been neatly done. Some skill, too, had been shown in the manner in which the limb had been removed from the trunk, but the handiwork was scarcely good enough for a person acquainted with the principles of anatomy. The flesh was comparatively fresh, and was not quite free from blood, but it appears to have been in the water two or three days. The arm had most probably been removed from the trunk after death, and it bore no bruises or sign of violent usage.

As soon as the medical examination had been concluded, Inspector Adams had the arm removed to the mortuary in Millbank-street, and then proceeded with his investigations. His first care was to have the whole of the river in the immediate neighbourhood thoroughly dragged. The work was continued until a late hour in the evening, but, according to the police, no more human remains were found. The police records of missing persons were also carefully searched, but they yielded nothing that could be described as a clue. On the 24th of last month a man who was sweeping the railway station at Guildford came across a parcel containing a human foot and leg, which he at once handed over to the local police. The parcel had apparently been thrown either from a passing train or from a bridge which passes over the railway close to where it was found. But it is not probable that the arm found yesterday had anything to do with the Guildford remains. The limb found yesterday was comparatively fresh; at any rate, it formed part of a living body not more than four days ago. Within the last week there has been reported to the police an average number of disappearances of women; but, as far as can be ascertained, not one of them can be connected with the present case.

It is possible, but not at all probable, that this arm may have been cut from the body of a young married woman, who left her home at Lewisham on the 20th ult., and has not since been heard of. She was twenty-three years of age, and tall; but she had threatened to commit suicide, and it is more likely that she carried out her threat than that she was the victim of a murderer. It is possible, also, that the arm may have been placed where found by some medical student, but this view is not shared by the authorities. Inquiries are, however, being made at the various hospitals and private medical schools, the result of which can scarcely be made known until to-day.

Daily Gazette for Middlesbrough - Wednesday 12 September 1888

THE LATEST MURDER.

A profound sensation was created late yesterday afternoon by a report that another fiendish murder had been committed, this time in the Western part of London. There is, unfortunately, too much reason to believe that the report will prove to be absolutely correct. A policeman's attention was attracted to something at which a number of boys were pelting stones in the Thames near Ebury Bridge. He had the object of the boys amusement extracted from the planks of timber amongst which it was entangled, and on examining it he found it to be a human arm. He had it at once removed to the Station, where it was inspected by Dr. Neville, of Pimlico road, the Police surgeon. The arm had been removed from the shoulder, and had evidently been done by an unskilful person. It must have been removed from the body of a person murdered but a day or two, as when touched the blood began to trickle freshly from it. The instrument must, too, have been exceedingly sharp, the joint being cut into, and the limb removed at the shoulder socket. There was a cord tied round the arm above the elbow. The person murdered must have been a very fine young woman. The arm was fully as long as that of a man of 5ft, 10in. or 5ft. 11in. This shows the woman must have been about 5ft. 8 in. There were a few abrasions on portions of the skin, but these might be caused by knocking against the timber in the water. The police have discovered no further remains, though a diligent watch has been kept at the river side. The arm already found is lying at the Millbank road mortuary, but it is not contemplated to hold an inquest at present, as other portions of the body may be discovered. A number of the river side habitues are likewise closely watching this morning.

Dundee Courier - Wednesday 12 September 1888

ANOTHER GHASTLY TRAGEDY IN LONDON. WOMAN MURDERED AND MUTILATED.

A profound sensation was created late yesterday afternoon by the publication of a report that another fiendish murder has been committed, this time in the western part of London. There is unfortunately too much reason to believe that the report will prove to be absolutely correct, and already the police are pursuing inquiries based upon this assumption. About twenty minutes to one yesterday afternoon a man named Frederick Moore, employed at Messrs Ward's timber yard, Grosvenor Road, had his attention drawn to a curious object lying on the mud on the banks of the Thames, immediately opposite where he was working. Moore procured a ladder and descended to the bank below the wharf. On approaching the object he was startled to find that it was a human arm. It was partly wedged between some timber in the wood dock belonging to Messrs Chappel. Moore's first thought was to secure the ghastly object so that it might not be carried away by the tide or current, and this object be ensured by tying it to a haulk of timber with some string which he had in his pocket. He then carefully examined the immediate vicinity, but failing to find any more human remains he took up the arm, carried it to the Embankment, and there handed it over to the care of Police Constable James, obtained a newspaper from a neighbouring publichouse, and having wrapped up the arm, which had already attracted the morbid curiosity of a rapidly gathering crowd, conveyed it to the Gerald Row Police Station. Inspector Adams, of the B.T. Division, at once took charge of the case, and his first care, after communicating the discovery to Scotland Yard, was to send for Dr Neville, of Pimlico Road and Sloane Street, the nearest medical man, who soon arrived at the Police Station, and made a most careful examination of the remains. He had no difficulty in deciding that the arm was that of a well-formed, tall, and well- nourished young woman, probably about 25 years of age. It had been cut off at the shoulder with some sharp instrument, and the question at once naturally suggested itself, “Is this the work of a professional anatomist or of a murderer?” Dr Neville did not feel called upon to express a positive opinion either way, but he could not deny that the work had been neatly done. Some skill too, had been shown in the manner in which the limb had been removed from the trunk, but the handiwork was scarcely good enough for a person acquainted with the principles anatomy. The flesh was comparatively fresh, and was not quite free from blood, but it had been in the water at least two or three days. The arm had been removed from the trunk, of course, after death, and it bore no bruises of signs of violent usage. As soon as the medical examination had been concluded, Inspector Adams had the arm removed to the mortuary in Millbank. He then proceeded with his investigations. His first care was to have the whole of the river in the immediate neighbourhood thoroughly dragged. The work was continued until a late hour in the evening, but, according to the police, no more human remains were found. The police records of missing persons were also carefully searched, but they yielded nothing that could be described as a clue. On the 24th of last month a man who was sweeping the Railway Station at Guildford came across a parcel containing a human foot and leg, which he at once handed over to the local police. The parcel had apparently been thrown either from a passing train or from a bridge which passes over the railway close to where it was found, but it is not probable that the arm found yesterday had anything to do with the Guildford remains, inasmuch as the latter were boiled, so much so that some of the flesh and the toenails had entirely disappeared from the bone. As already stated, the limb found yesterday was comparatively fresh - at any rate, it formed part of a living body not more than four days ago. Within the last week there has been reported to the police an average number of mysterious disappearances of women, but, as far as can be ascertained, not one of them can be connected with the present case. It is possible, but not at all probable, that the mysterious arm may have been cut from the body of a young married woman who left her home at Lewisham on the 20th ult., and has not since been heard of. She was 23 years of age, and tall, but she had threatened to commit suicide, and it is more likely that she carried out her threat than that she was the victim of a murder. Coming nearer to date the body of a woman apparently between forty and fifty years of age was found floating off Lambeth on Monday morning, and it has not yet been identified, but the corpse was that of a spare woman about four feet three inches high. It is possible that the arm may have been placed where found by some medical student or other practical joker, but this view is not shared by the authorities. Inquiries are, however, being made at the various hospitals and private medical schools, the result of which can scarcely be made known until to-day.

Frederick Moore, of 86 Great Peter Street, Westminster, informed a reporter that he is a deal porter, and works at Mr Ward's timber yard at Grosvenor Road, Westminster. He gives the following account of the discovery :- "ln the dinner hour yesterday, about twenty minutes to one, I was standing outside the yard talking to one of the clerks, when my attention was drawn by some of my fellow workmen to something lying on the mud inside the floating timber belonging to Messrs ChappeL I went over and looked at it, then said, 'Oh, that is nothing.' I then went away, and was crossing the road, when I was called back, and asked to fetch a hitcher, a kind of hook used for hauling about the timber. Not being able to find a hitcher in the yard I took a 20 feet rod, but being unable to reach the object with this rod another man went and got a ladder. We hoisted the ladder over the embankment on the floating timber. There was a short ladder lying upon the timber, and I pushed this ladder out over the mud until I was able to reach the object, which I then saw was an arm. It had a flat piece of string or tape tied round the upper part over the muscle, and the knuckle bone of the shoulder was protruding from the flesh about an inch or so. It had been cut off just below the shoulder. When I first saw the arm it was lying on the mud with the fingers pointing out to the river. About two or three months ago I picked up the dead body of a child near the place where I picked up the arm yesterday."

Shields Daily Gazette - Thursday 13 September 1888

THE PIMLICO MYSTERY.
DR. NEVILLE'S OPINION.

Yesterday afternoon Dr. Thomas Neville, divisional surgeon, visited the mortuary at Ebury Bridge, Pimlico, for the purpose of minutely examining the arm found in the Thames on Tuesday. The limb will for the present remain at the mortuary, awaiting the orders of Mr Troutbeck, the district coroner, who has been officially informed of the discovery, but it is improbable that an inquest will be held. The Thames police are making every endeavour to find other portions of the body, if any, in the river, and officers of the Criminal Investigation Department are making inquiries. The authorities still believe that a murder has been committed.

INTERVIEW WITH THE DOCTOR

A reporter has interviewed Dr. Neville, who examined the arm found in the Thames on Tuesday.

Were there any rings on the hands, doctor? asked the reporter. -- No; and no signs of rings having been worn that I could see.

Was there anything to indicate whether the arm was that of a woman of refinement or the reverse? -- Well, I should say not a refined woman, for the ails were dirty.

That might be due to immersion in the dirty water of the river? – Certainly; but I also observed that the nails were not neatly trimmed as a lady's generally are.

Can you say whether the woman was dark or fair? – Fair, because the hair on the arm was fair.

By-the-bye, I suppose there is no doubt that it is a woman's arm and not a man's? – Oh, I think not. The contour of the arm, the shape of the hand, and the delicacy of the whole limb told me that it was a woman's.

A young woman's or that of an elderly person? – No doubt that of a young woman – under 30 years I should say, judging from the freshness of the skin and the tension of the muscles and sinews.

Now, what is your idea about the cord? – It is difficult to say what the cord was tied around the arm for, unless it was to prevent blood from flowing from the limb while it was conveyed to the water. It was tied near the end of the arm not far from the cut, and undoubtedly would have had the effect of keeping the blood from running down out of the hand.

Could this limb possibly have come from some dissecting room? – I do not think so for a moment. If it had there would have been on it some evidence of the dissection. The object of surgical dissection would, of course, be to see the development of the muscles and so on, but the way in which this limb has been severed prevents anything of the sort being seen. Moreover, no dissecting-room authorities would allow the removal of a limb.

Then this discovery could not be due to some medical student's freak? – I consider that explanation of the matter an impossible one. The limb must have been severed with a large sharp knife, whereas a dissecting knife is a small one.

Can you say whether the owner of the limb was dead or alive when it was severed from the shoulder? – It is difficult to say with certainty, of course, but my opinion is that the person must have been dead very recently when the arm was cut off.

By recently, do you mean a day or two? – Yes, or less than that.

Does the member give you an idea of what sort of woman it belonged to? – She would be a woman 5 feet 8 inches in height, stout, well built, well proportioned, and well nourished.

Then this is not an arm to be accounted for by a surgical amputation? – No, it has not been removed skilfully enough. This dismemberment seems to have been done without any object except the removal of the arm from the shoulder, for what reason of course I cannot fathom. It certainly to me suggests murder. I cannot imagine in what other light to regard it. The muscles were clean cut through, so that the knife used must have been very sharp, and the bone was wrenched from the socket.

South Wales Daily News - Thursday 13 September 1888

THE PIMLICO MYSTERY.
STARTLING REVELATIONS ANTICIPATED.
EXTRAORDINARY THEORIES.
THE DISCOVERY OF BOILED REMAINS AT GUILDFORD.

The discovery of human remains at Pimlico has created a profound sensation, and the wildest rumours are already afloat as to whether another hideous crime, even more mysterious than the Whitechapel murders, has or has not been perpetrated in the West-end of London. There are believed to be some startling features in connection with the case which cannot at present be revealed, as officials are now engaged in making their investigation into this the latest London mystery. No portions of any body have been missed from any of the London hospitals, and such are the stringent regulations applying to dissection that it is considered impossible for a single limb to be clandestinely conveyed out of the hospital without its absence being immediately detected. Inspector Adams, Inspector Arthur Hare, Inspector Kendrick, and other officers are busy making inquiries at certain localities in Pimlico; while diligent search is being made along the banks of the Thames for any other human remains as it is thought not improbable that the remaining portions of the woman's trunk - presuming the case to be one of murder - will be sooner or later discovered.

In the meantime several theories are advanced as to this mysterious affair. One is that the poor woman died from the effects of an unlawful operation committed in some house of evil repute; that her body was then cut up, in order to first of all conceal the crime, and, secondly, to the more easily disposal of it; and that it was the work of a man having medical knowledge. Another theory is that the deceased has been killed by the same unseen hand that committed the dastardly crimes in Whitechapel, and that the arm has actually been brought from the East-end to Pimlico, in order to throw the police off the scent. Inspector Abberline, Inspector Helson, Inspector Reid, and other officers engaged in investigating the Whitechapel crimes have been in communication with Scotland-yard with reference to the finding of the arm, but no clue has as yet been found.

Dr Neville is of opinion that the woman met her death about three days ago, and that the limb was cut off soon after the poor creature's decease. The police records of missing persons have been carefully searched, but they yielded nothing that could be described as a clue. On the 21st of last month a man who was sweeping the railway station at Guildford came across a parcel containing a human foot and leg, which he at once handed over to the local police. The parcel had apparently been thrown either from a passing train or from a bridge which passes over the railway close to where it was found. But it is not probable that the arm bad anything to do with the Guildford remains, inasmuch as the latter were boiled - so much so, that some of the flesh and the toe-nails had entirely disappeared from the bones.

St James's Gazette - Thursday 13 September 1888

THE PIMLICO MYSTERY.

Careful consideration of all the circumstances connected with the finding of the human arm in the Thames as narrated yesterday have strengthened the belief that there is a crime at the bottom of this mystery. Dr. Neville is most emphatic in his declaration that the arm has not been severed from the body for "scientific purposes," and this would seem to dispose of the idea that the throwing of the limb into the Thames is part of a joke on the part of medical students for the purpose of heightening the public alarm at a particular moment. The most diligent search is being made on land and water. It is to be remembered that the Richmond murder was a case of the same character, and the horrible murder and mutilation perpetrated by one low woman was enveloped in mystery for some days until a clue was obtained, which, followed up by the police, led to the unravelling of the whole story.

Belfast News-Letter - Thursday 13 September 1888

THE PIMLICO MYSTERY

LONDON, WEDNESDAY. – The Central News says:- The Thames police were engaged for several hours this afternoon in dragging the river between the Pimlico steamboat pier and the London, Brighton, and South Coast Railway bridge, between which points the arm of a woman was found yesterday. A careful examination was also made of the timber rafts floating in the river, but no discovery of human remains was made. It is the opinion of the river police that the arm was dropped over the Embankment, which at night is darker than most thoroughfares owing to the numerous trees no in full leaf, and little frequented. The arm is still in the mortuary, and will be further examined by surgical experts. In regard to the theory that the arm might have been thrown onto the river bank by a medical student with a view to create a scare, a representative of the Central News called at one of the chief London hospitals to-day. He was assured that the arm could not possibly have been removed by a student from any hospital dissecting room. Students are allowed to dissect only in the rooms set apart for the purpose. Under the act of William the Fourth hospitals and medical schools are allowed to receive unclaimed bodies for the purposes of dissection, but forty-eight hours' notice has to be given after death to the inspector under the act before the body can be removed from the place, and then only after a certificate of death has been given. The bodies, if being dissected, must be buried in consecrated ground, and within six weeks a certificate of burial must be forwarded to the inspector. Under no circumstances are students allowed to take portions of bodies to their own houses. In fact, they would be liable under the act to a heavy penalty for doing so.

London Daily News - Friday 14 September 1888

THE SUPPOSED MUTILATION IN PIMLICO
A YOUNG WOMAN MISSING

A Mrs. Potter, living in Spencer-buildings, Westminster, applied to Mr. d'Eyncourt, at Westminster Police-court, yesterday afternoon, stating that she had reason to fear that the arm found in the river off Grosvenor-road belonged to her daughter Emma, a girl 17 years of age, of rather weak intellect, who had been missing from home since Saturday morning, at 11 o'clock. Her daughter had given her some trouble by frequenting the streets at night, and at this time of the year it was particularly troublesome. At two o'clock on Saturday morning a policeman brought her home, and applicant at eleven o'clock in the forenoon went out, leaving her asleep on a couch. On her return her daughter had gone, and from that time she had seen nothing of her, although she had diligently made inquiries and been to places – the Green Park in particular – where she knew the girl was likely to go. She had been to workhouses and infirmaries without success, and the only item of information she could gain was from a policeman who had known the girl by sight. He last saw her at half-past five on Saturday evening near Buckingham-gate. Applicant said she had been that morning to see Dr. Neville, the acting divisional surgeon of police, and he remarked that the particulars she gave him of her daughter could in every way correspond to the arm which had been found. The doctor questioned her particularly as to the stature and appearance of her daughter, and, having given his opinion, referred her to the police. The applicant, who was referred by the magistrate to the Press, furnished the following description of the missing girl: Tall and well formed, and of rather dark complexion, long arms, and a short nail on the left hand; attired in a brown dress, black jacket, white hat with black velvet band and white lace in front, high lace-up boots.

Western Mail - Friday 14 September 1888

TIHE PIMILICO MYSTERY.
THE POLICE PUZZLED.
SUPPOSED TO BE ANOTHER WHITECHAPEL MURDER.

Scotland Yard is puzzled to no ordinary degree by the discovery made at a Pimlico wharf, where a woman's arm was picked out of the Thames, under circumstances already reported. Several experienced detectives have worked indefatigably, but the entire absence of any clue, either as regards identification of the body from which the arm was severed or of the person who threw the limb into the Thames, has rendered their efforts abortive, and up to noon on Thursday nothing in any way eliciting evidence has come to the knowledge of the police authorities, nor has any other portion of the human remains yet been discovered. The limb could not, it is thought, have been cut from a corpse legitimately dissected. The anatomical schools are now, it is stated, in vacation. On Wednesday all the Metropolitan and suburban hospitals were visited, but nothing could be gained to throw any light on the case. On the contrary, it seems to be established almost beyond a doubt that the arm did not come from any recognised London medical institution. A further medical examination has proved that the arm was not cut from a living woman. It, too, was not - judging from its appearance - severed by a skilled hand in performing a surgical operation. The theory mentioned in the *Echo* on Wednesday - that some young woman died from the effects of unlawful treatment, and that her body was then cut up - is to a large extent accepted by the Criminal Investigation officers; "but," as one authority said on Thursday morning, "we might have to search every house in London, respectable or not, before we could get the slightest evidence in that way."

Various applications in respect to missing female friends have since the announcement of the discovery of the arm been made at the Gerald-road Police-station. These cases have been, and are still being, inquired into. Amongst the East End detectives an opinion still prevails that the unfortunate woman was murdered in Whitechapel, and her body cut up there.

Lancashire Evening Post - Friday 14 September 1888

ANOTHER LONDON MYSTERY CLEARED UP.

Inspector Webster, A Division, attended before the magistrate at Westminster, to-day, and stated that the police, last night, found and took home the girl Emma Potter, who was reported missing by her mother, who had expressed the fear that the girl's disappearance might be associated with the discovery of a mutilated arm at Pimlico.

Wrexham Advertiser - Saturday 15 September 1888

HORRIBLE DISCOVERY AT PIMLICO ANOTHER WOMAN MUTILATED.

Yet another outrage has to be added to the list of undiscovered crimes which have recently startled the inhabitants of the metropolis. On Tuesday, soon after noon, the attention of several persons passing along Grosvenor Road, Pimlico, was drawn to what appeared to be a portion of a human body floating in the River Thames near Grosvenor Railway Bridge. It is stated that the object was first seen entangled among some timber floating on the riverside, and that a number of boys, imagining it to be the carcase of a drowned dog, amused themselves by pelting it with stones. Upon closer examination, however, it proved to be a human arm. The police were at once sent for, and a constable who was on duty near the spot took charge of the limb, which he conveyed to the police station at Gerald Road, Eaton Square. Dr. Thomas Neville, surgeon, of 85, Pimlico Road, and of 123, Sloane Street, subsequently made an examination of the arm, and, though he has made no official report on the subject at present, there is every reason to believe that another piece of foul play has been brought to light. It appears that the limb which has been discovered is the right arm of a female, probably of some twenty-five or thirty years of age. It has been severed at the shoulder-joint, and has the appearance of having been in the water some two or three days. The cut was not skilfully made, and was such as would be the case had the operation been performed by a person ignorant of the elements of anatomy. Round the arm and above the elbow was a piece of string, tied somewhat tightly, but not sufficiently taut to produce much of an indentation. It is thought not unlikely that the string may have been employed to prevent the blood oozing through the veins, and so causing a risk of splashing to the person disposing of the severed limb. If this was the intention the artifice was scarcely successful, as when taken from the river there was still some bleeding. Another conjecture is that the string was merely attached for the purpose of easy carriage. At any rate, this was the idea which struck the police-constable, who carried the limb to the police-station by means of another piece of string attached to that already round the remains.

The contour of the limb, the delicacy of the hand, and the want of muscular development clearly indicate that the arm is that of a woman, and that comparatively young. It is difficult, of course, to tell the precise age, but the examination showed that the female, whoever she was, was a well-developed person, apparently in good health. There was no trace of disease of any kind, and there were no bruises suggestive of violence, but there were one or two slight abrasions, caused probably by contact with bridges or floating timber. It is not easy to say when the limb was cut off, but Dr. Neville, we understand, inclines to the view that the knife was used very soon after death. Had the act been performed some considerable time after death the appearance of the limb would have indicated it. The suggestion was put forward that the limb probably came from a dissecting-room; but the character of the cut negatives any such theory. The arm was evidently cut through by a big, sharp instrument, compared with which the ordinary dissecting-room knife is a mere toy. Moreover, the merest tyro in the dissecting-room would not think of amputating a limb in this fashion. The theory which the police are forced to entertain is that the arm forms part of a woman who has met with a tragic end, and whose body is being disposed of in sections as opportunity offers. The single limb which after examination was taken to the mortuary at Ebury Bridge, affords, however no clue upon which the police authorities can act. What they have done is to order a careful search of the river for any other portions of the remains, and should these be discovered by the river police identification may be possible. So far the police see no reason to connect the discovery with any of the cases of mysterious disappearance frequently reported to them: although the remains were found in the river off Pimlico, they do not at present associate the supposed crime with any particular district. At the time of this discovery it was about low water. The dismembered limb may therefore have floated down from Richmond or from Chelsea. On the other hand, the preceding flood-tide may have sent it up the river from Woolwich or Wapping. All that can be said is that the Thames has yielded up evidence of another horrible deed, committed certainly within the last two or three days.

Pall Mall Gazette - Friday 28 September 1888

THE PIMLICO MYSTERY.
ANOTHER DISCOVERY.

A discovery was made in Southwark this morning which is supposed to have some connection with what is known as the Pimlico Mystery. Some time ago, it will be remembered, the arm of a woman, sharply cut off from the body, was found in the Thames at Pimlico, but all the efforts of the police to discover any other portions of the body were attended with no success. This morning, between seven and eight o'clock, a boy was passing the Blind School in the Lambeth-road. There is a garden attached to the school, enclosed by iron railways. Inside these railings the boy noticed a curiously shaped parcel lying on the grass. He fished it out, and found to his astonishment that it contained a woman's arm. It was somewhat decomposed, and had been placed in lime. The parcel was given over to the police, and the supposition is that the limb was cut from the same body as that which was found in the Thames at Pimlico.

London Evening Standard - Saturday 29 September 1888

HORRIBLE DISCOVERY IN SOUTHWARK.

About half-past seven o'clock yesterday morning, a horrible discovery was made in Southwark, which tallies with the late discovery at Pimlico. lt appears that a lad was walking along the Lambeth-road, and, passing the Blind School, which has a garden protected by railings, ne noticed a curiously-shaped paper parcel lying on the grass inside the railings. The lad obtained possession of the parcel, and on opening it found it to contain the arm of a woman. It was somewhat decomposed, and had lime thrown over it. The attention of a policeman of the L division was called, and the limb was given into his charge. A bricklayer, named Jim Moore, said to a reporter:- "At about a quarter-past seven this morning I was walking along Lambeth-road, when I saw a boy pick up a parcel through the railings which surround the Blind School. He was opening it when I went up, and saw the arm of a young woman, which had been put in lime." The licensed shoeblack who stands at the corner of a public-house facing the Blind School, said:- "Seeing some people round a parcel which had been fished out of the garden, I went over. The parcel lay opened, and I saw the arm of a woman which had been cut from the body. It was decomposed, and had been laid in lime. The fingers were clutched."

Pall Mall Gazette - Monday 01 October 1888

THE DISCOVERY OF HUMAN REMAINS.

All doubt as to whether a discovery of human remains had been made on Friday near the Blind School in Lambeth-road was set at rest on Saturday by the admission of the Southwark coroner, Mr. S. F. Langham, that such a discovery had been reported to him by the police. Sensational reports were in circulation both on Friday and Saturday that the parcel found contained a woman's arm, with portions of the flesh still remaining upon it. These statements led to the further report that the discovery was connected with the recent Pimlico mystery, and the reticence of the police in giving information respecting the matter naturally increased the suspicion; but an investigation in quarters where the actual facts were well known shows conclusively that, while the entire skeleton of an arm, from the shoulder-blade to the fingers, was found wrapped up in some canvas, there is no foundation whatever for the story as to there being flesh upon it. It has evidently been dug up after a long interment in the ground.

Yorkshire Post and Leeds Intelligencer - Monday 01 October 1888

THE PIMLICO MYSTERY.

At the conclusion of several inquests which were held on Saturday morning at Guy's Hospital a question was addressed to the coroner (Mr. S. F. Langham) as to whether the alleged finding of a human arm in Lambeth Road had been brought to his knowledge in an official way, so that the truth of the statement that such a discovery had or had not been made might be authoritatively settled. Mr. Langham at once replied that he had that morning received a police notice informing him that such a discovery had been made, but whether the notice had emanated from the police at Stonesend Station or from Kensington Road he could not remember. Inquiries made subsequently showed that portions of an arm were conveyed to the mortuary on Friday, wrapped in a piece of dirty canvas, and tied round with string. The parcel contained the skeleton of a portion of an arm, extending from the elbow to the fingers. It is not now believed to have any connection with the discovery made at Pimlico.

Hull Daily Mail - Wednesday 03 October 1888

THE SHOCKING DISCOVERY AT WESTMINSTER.

The Press Association says the inhabitants of Westminster appear to have only this morning realised the horrible nature of the crime exposed yesterday in their midst and details of the ghastly discovery in Whitehall are to-day discussed by everyone with horrified eagerness. The official investigation into the cause of the victim's death was commenced at an early hour. Dr Bond, divisional police surgeon, and Dr Hibbert, his assistant, arrived at the mortuary shortly after 7 a.m. The mortuary is temporarily placed at an untenanted shop and house, 20 Millbank street, and the body was removed there at seven o'clock on Tuesday night, and placed in spirits. The doctors' examination of the trunk lasted for about an hour and a half, and proved a most unpleasant task, owing to the advanced stage of decomposition of the flesh. – Dr Bond would not state what the result of the examination was until after he has made his official report, which would be immediately; but he stated that it was intended to obtain the arm which was found in the Thames on the 11th September, and which has since been preserved at the Ebury-street Mortuary in order to ascertain whether it had been taken from the same trunk. – An inquest will probably be held, but this will depend upon the nature of Dr Bond's report to the coroner, Dr Troutbeck – The detectives were also early on the scene, and resumed their inquiries among workmen employed at the works where the discovery was made. It has been ascertained that the parcel containing the remains was not in the vault on Saturday, as several of the workmen had been in the habit of using the cellar to conceal their tools, and it would have been noticed. As it was, the parcel was first seen on Monday morning, but none of the workmen had the curiosity to look what was in it until Tuesday, when it was dragged out with the result already known. A search is now being made in the cellars and the disused well for any other portion of the remains.

The Press Association learns that Mr Troutbeck has decided to hold an inquest on the remains, but the date is not yet fixed, and will probably not be for three days at least. Detectives are still employed searching round the scene of the discovery this afternoon. There are indications that the hoarding surrounding the works has recently been scaled.

The police have since thoroughly inspected the clothing attached to the body with the object of ascertaining if there were any blood stains, but the result of this examination has not transpired. The inquest has been fixed for Monday next.

THE SURGEON'S OPINION

The Press Association learns this afternoon that the surgeons who examined the remains have come to the conclusion that the arm which was found at Pimlico fitted into the trunk found on Tuesday.

London Evening Standard - Wednesday 03 October 1888

SHOCKING DISCOVERY IN WESTMINSTER.

About three o'clock yesterday afternoon a shocking discovery was made in a vault beneath the buildings of the New Central Police Offices, Cannon-row, Westminster, the site of the Opera House which it was some years since proposed to construct on the Victoria-embankment. A labourer engaged upon the works noticed a large bundle tied up with cord, and drew the attention of the assistant foreman to it, who ordered him to pull it out and untie it. Upon doing so he found wrapped up in an old black skirt the trunk of a human being much decomposed. The police at King-street Police-station were at once communicated with, and Inspector Marshall, from the Criminal Investigation

Department, took charge of the remains, and immediately summoned a doctor. Upon a close examination it was found that the intestines were slightly protruding. The arms, the legs, and the head had been cut off, and were missing. Nothing in the shape of clothing beyond the black skirt referred to covered the remains, which are those of a female of about 25 years of age, so far as it was possible to judge. The doctor gave orders for the remains to be preserved in spirits, and the Coroner's officer having been apprised of the discovery, they were removed to the mortuary in Millbank-street to await an inquest. An opinion was expressed that the body had probably been dead for about a month.

The spot where the discovery was made is at the extreme end of a long subway of vaults, which are being constructed for store-rooms, and the bundle was deposited in a dark recess, about 100 yards from the roadway. The workmen engaged there state that, in their belief, it must have been left there between Saturday and Monday last, and one man asserts that he saw the bundle on Monday, but passed it, thinking it was probably some old rags dug up out of the excavations. Minute search is being made all over the works for the remaining portions of the body. Already some pieces of black material corresponding with the black skirt in which the body was wrapped have been collected from other parts of the premises, and they appear to be portions of the same covering.

On the discovery becoming known hundreds of persons congregated throughout the afternoon and evening discussing the matter, the rumour having spread that the Whitechapel murders had been repeated in the neighbourhood. The general belief is that the trunk forms part of the same body, the limbs of which were recently found in Pimlico.

Dr. Nevill, who examined the arm of a female found a few weeks ago in the Thames, off Ebury Bridge, said on that occasion that he did not think that it had been skilfully taken from the body, and this fact would appear to favour the theory that that arm, together with the one found in the grounds of the Blind Asylum in the Lambeth-road last week, belong to the trunk discovered yesterday, for it is stated that the limbs appear to have been taken from the body in anything but a skilful manner.

Another account says:- A further addition to the annals of crime was brought to light yesterday afternoon, the scene on this occasion being within a stone's throw of the Houses of Parliament. At a few minutes after four o'clock a human body, mutilated in a most revolting manner, was discovered in an unfinished building on the Thames Embankment. Intense excitement prevailed last night in the neighbourhood on the fact becoming known, and for several hours groups of persons gathered together discussing the subject, for the past twelve months the new police-offices, in place of those at Scotland-yard, have been in course of erection, the site being that on the Embankment on which the Opera House was to have been built. The contractors are Mesrs. J. Grover and Sons, of Wilton Works, New North-road, and the building was advancing rapidly. A large number of hands are employed; but it was never deemed necessary to engage a night watchman. In addition to a lengthy hoarding on the Embankment, which is fifteen or sixteen feet in height, there is another hoarding of a similar description running along Canon-row, a thoroughfare leading out of Parliament-street, and running directly at the rear of the Embankment. This was the direct approach to the works, temporary gateways being erected for the purpose. The basement and other parts of the building were completed, the former containing a number of vaults. Several of these are described as being extremely dark in one corner. In fulfilling their duties the workmen frequently passed to and fro, but observed nothing particular to attract their attention.

On Monday morning the foreman, in making his rounds, happened to glance in a corner of one of the vaults, obscured from view, and about sixty or seventy yards from the principal gate in Canon-row, but comparatively out of reach of the Embankment. His eye alighted on a dark-looking object, which had the appearance of an old coat, and which he believed had been thrown there by one of the workmen. Yesterday afternoon, two or three pieces of black or dark material, used for ladies' dresses, were discovered in different parts of the works, and he sent a labourer to get the parcel he had seen in the vault. On bringing it to the light the men were horrified, and the stench arising from it almost overcame them. The covering was of the same material as that previously spoken of, but it was tied with cord. On removing the fastenings a mutilated trunk was exhibited, the head, arms, and legs being cut away. The body itself was further bound with cords, but was frightfully decomposed. From its appearance it was that of a woman of somewhat full proportions. The foreman immediately communicated with the police at King-street station, and, in a few minutes, Inspectors Peter and Marshall arrived, accompanied by other officers. Information of the discovery was also conveyed to Dr. Bond, who in turn directed Dr. Hibbert to attend. The latter gentleman made a brief examination, and at once pronounced the remains to be those of a woman.

After a more minute investigation the medical gentleman is stated to have expressed an idea that the woman had been dismembered by an unskilful person, and further, he was fully of opinion that the arm found at Pimlico belonged to the same individual. A fuller examination, however, will be made this morning in conjunction with Dr. Bond.

After further investigation, it became apparent that the body must have been carried bodily and placed in the position in which it was found. It is impossible for anything to lodge in such a manner if thrown over the hoarding on the Embankment, and it would be equally difficult for any person to climb over at that part, in order to gain access to the vault.

The police at present are completely in the dark as to the method adopted in gaining access to the building, but they incline to the opinion that it is the act of some one fully cognisant of the arrangements.

Pall Mall Gazette - Wednesday 03 October 1888

ANOTHER GHASTLY DISCOVERY IN LONDON.
A MUTILATED BODY AT WESTMINSTER.

About twenty minutes past three o'clock yesterday afternoon Frederick Wildborn, a carpenter employed by Messrs. J. Grover and Sons, builders, of Pimlico, who are the contractors for the new Metropolitan Police headquarters on the Thames Embankment, was working on the foundation, when he came across a neatly done up parcel in one of the cellars. It was opened, and the body of a woman, very much decomposed, was found carefully wrapped in a piece of what is supposed to be a black petticoat. The trunk was without head, arms, or legs, and presented a horrible spectacle. Dr. Bond, the divisional surgeon, and several other medical gentlemen were communicated with, and from what can be ascertained the conclusion has been arrived at by them that these remains are those of a woman whose arms have recently been discovered in different parts of the metropolis. Dr. Nevill, who examined the arm of a woman found a few weeks ago in the Thames, off Ebury Bridge, said on that occasion that he did not think that it had been skilfully taken from the body. This fact would appear to favour the theory that that arm, together with the one found I in the grounds of the Blind Asylum in the Lambeth-road last week, belong to the trunk discovered yesterday, for it is stated that the limbs appear to have been taken from it in anything but a skilful manner.

The building which is in course of erection is the new police depot for London. The builders have been working on the site for some time now, but have only just completed the foundation. It was originally the site for the National Opera-house, and extends from the Thames Embankment through Cannon-row, Parliament-street, at the back of St. Stephen's Club and the Westminster Bridge-station on the District Railway. The prevailing opinion is that to place the body where it was found the person conveying it must have scaled the 8 ft. hoarding which encloses the works, and, carefully avoiding the watchmen who do duty by night, must have dropped it where it was found. The body could not have been where it was found above two or three days, because men are frequently passing the spot. One of the workmen says that it was not there last Friday, because they had occasion to do something at that very spot. It is thought that the person who put the bundle there could not very well have got into the enclosure from the Embankment side, as not only would the risk of detection be very great, but he would stand a good chance of breaking his neck. The parcel must have been got in from the Cannon-row side, a very dark and lonely spot, although within twenty yards of the main thoroughfare. The body is pronounced by medical men to have been that of a remarkably fine young woman. The lower portion from the ribs has been removed. The postmortem examination was held this morning and the result will be made known at the inquest.

Dundee Courier - Wednesday 03 October 1888

ANOTHER LONDON HORROR.
DISCOVERY OF A WOMAN'S MUTILATED BODY.
PANIC IN THE METROPOLIS.
LATEST PARTICULARS.

The Press Association says:- Another ghastly discovery was made in London yesterday afternoon. About twenty minutes past three o'clock yesterday afternoon a carpenter named Frederick Wildburn, employed by Messrs J. Grover & Sons, builders, of Pimlico, who are the contractors for the New Metropolitan Police Headquarters on the Thames Embankment, was working on the foundation, when he came across a neatly done-up parcel, which was secreted in one of the cellars. Wildburn was in search of timber when he found the parcel, which was tied up in paper, and measured about two-and-a-half feet long by about two feet in width. It was opened, and the body of a woman very much decomposed was found, carefully wrapped in a piece of cloth, which is supposed to be a black petticoat. The trunk was minus the head, both arms and both legs, and presented a ghastly spectacle. The officials of the works were immediately apprised of the discovery, and the police were fetched. Dr Bond, the divisional surgeon to the A Division, and several other medical gentlemen were communicated with, and subsequently examined the remains, which were handed over to the care of some police officers, who were told off to see that it was not disturbed. From what can be ascertained the conclusion has been arrived at by the medical men that these remains are those of the woman whose arms have recently been discovered in different parts of the Metropolis. Dr Nevill, who examined the arm of a female found a few weeks ago in the Thames off Ebury Bridge, said on that occasion that he did not think it had been skilfully taken from the body, and this fact would appear to favour the theory that the arm, together with the one found in the grounds of the Blind Asylum in the Lambeth Road last week, belong to the trunk discovered yesterday, for it is stated that the limbs appear to have been taken from the body found yesterday afternoon in anything but a skilful manner. The building, which is in course of erection, is the new police depot for London, the present scattered headquarters of the Metropolitan police force and the Criminal Investigation Department in Great Scotland Yard and Whitehall Place having been found too small for the requirements of our police system. The builders have been working on the site for some considerable time now, but have only just completed the foundation. It was originally the site for the National Opera House, and extends from the Thames Embankment through to Cannon Row, Parliament Street, at the back of St Stephen's Club and the Westminster Bridge Station on the District Railway. The prevailing opinion is that to place the body where it was found, the person conveying it must have scaled the eight foot hoarding which encloses the works, and carefully avoiding the watchmen who do duty by night, must have dropped it where it was found. There appears to be little doubt that the parcel had been in a cellar for some considerable time.

PERSONAL STATEMENTS.

A man employed upon the works, who was one of the first to see the remains, made the following statement to a representative of the press:- I went down into one of the cellars, which is about 20 feet by 15 feet in size, to look round, when I saw a parcel lying in a corner as though it had been thrown there carelessly. I might say that the cellar is really a part of the half finished basement of what are to be the new Police Offices. The parcel was a paper one which could easily be carried under the arm. When the parcel was opened I saw that it contained the trunk of a woman wrapped up in a coarse cloth. In cutting off the legs a portion of the abdomen had been cut away. The head and arms were also cut off close to the trunk. The police have been digging up rubbish, and any place where it seems likely any more remains could be hidden, but I don't think they have found anything more. The contents of the parcel were very much decomposed, and looked to me as though they had been in the place where they were found for three weeks or a month. My opinion is that the person, putting the parcel where it was found, must have got over the hoarding in Cannon Row and then thrown the bundle down.

Another workman says that the parcel was discovered by a man whom he only knows by the name of "George," who went down to get some timber. In his opinion the parcel had been there for quite three weeks, as it was terribly decomposed.

Another workman, who has a thorough knowledge of the facts connected with the finding of the ghastly remains, has made the following statement:- As one of our carpenters was putting away his tools at about five o'clock last (Monday) night in one of the vaults which are to form the foundation of the main building of the new offices which are to accommodate the police, he saw what seemed to be a heap of paper. As it is very dark in this particular spot, even during the day, the matter somehow did not appear to strike him as curious or out of the way, his passing thoughts being that it was merely a bundle of canvas which was being used on the works. He consequently mentioned the matter to no one, and having left his tools, came away and went home, thinking no more about the mysterious parcel which was to reveal another dreadful crime, probably perpetrated within a hundred yards of King Street Police Station, about two or three hundred yards from the present offices of the Criminal Investigation Department, and within fifty yards of the Houses of Parliament. Yesterday morning when be went to fetch his tools he became aware of a very peculiar smell proceeding from the dark corner, but at the time made no attempts to ascertain the cause. The matter, however, had taken possession of his mind, and later on in the day he mentioned the circumstance to one or two of his fellow workmen. They at once decided to tell the foreman. This was done, and the foreman, accompanied by some of the men, proceeded to the spot. One of the labourers was called to shift the parcel. It was then opened, and the onlookers were horrified to find that it contained a human body. The legs, arms, and head were missing, and the body presented a most sickening spectacle. It had evidently been dead for many days, as decomposition was far advanced. I never saw such a dreadful sight in my life; and the smell was dreadful. After we had got over the first surprise and nausea, we sent for the police, and a doctor was also sent for. We could see that the body was that of a full-grown woman, and when the doctor came he said the same thing. Almost immediately after that Dr Bond, of the Middlesex Hospital, came and saw the body.

ANOTHER ACCOUNT.

The Central News says:- We are officially authorised to confirm the report of the discovery of a human trunk on the Thames Embankment. The discovery was made by a man in the employ of the builder who has secured the contract for the erection of the new police headquarters upon the site of the abortive National Opera House speculation. The man had occasion to go into a vaulted cellar which was built by the contractor for the Opera House some years ago. He was first startled by the horrible stench which filled the place, and which caused him to look around to see whence it came. To his horror he saw a large mass of decomposed flesh, which, on closer observation, proved to be the headless, armless, legless trunk of a female. The workman rushed into the open air, called loudly for assistance, and then hurried for a policeman, who arrived almost immediately. Word was at once sent to Scotland Yard, and Dr Bond, divisional surgeon, and several other leading officials were quickly on the spot. The remains were conveyed in an ambulance stretcher to the Millbank Street Mortuary, Westminster, after which the vault was very carefully searched, with what success is not yet known. At the mortuary Dr Bond made a cursory examination of the remains. He found the cords had been tightly bound round the body, apparently with the idea of keeping it together when decomposition had fully set in. The trunk was wrapped in a coarse kind of cloth, which has, of course, been carefully preserved, and which may prove of the greatest importance in the work of solving the mystery of this the latest, and, perhaps, not the least horrible, of the crimes of this Metropolis. The police took possession of the remains, and gave orders that no stranger was to be admitted to the enclosure. How long do I think it possible the body could have been lying there? Well, it could not have been where we found it above two or three days, because men are frequently passing the spot. The place is very dark, and it is possible that it might have escaped notice on that account, but I know for a fact that it was not there last Friday, because we had occasion to do something at that very spot. Asked for his opinion as to how the parcel got into such a curious place, our informant seemed quite taken aback at the simplicity of the question, but said that he could not possibly conceive. The person who put the bundle there could not very well have got into the enclosure from the Embankment side, as not only would the risk of detection be very great, but he would stand a good chance of breaking his neck.

A MYSTERY HOW IT CAME THERE.

The Central News says:- The general appearance of the trunk indeed indicated that it bad been carefully placed where it was subsequently found. It is simply astounding that any man could have carried such an offensive burden through the public street without attracting attention, and it is still more extraordinary how it could have been taken into the vault without discovery. The route from Cannon Row to the vault is a difficult one. A hoarding some seven or eight feet high would have to be climbed, and the ground is of a very broken character. From the Embankment side the hoarding is about the same height, and to reach the vault one must actually pass through the building in course of erection, and round it, about which several policemen are constantly patrolling. It is more reasonable to assume that the vault was gained from Cannon Row, and in that case it seems certain more than one person was concerned in the disposal of the ghastly parcel. One man probably climbed to the top of the hoarding with the assistance of his accomplice, from where he then received the parcel, dropped it on the inner side, and then let himself down after it. The other man, presumably, kept watch while his confederate disposed of the remains. How the men could have known of the existence of the vault is not clear, for strangers are not admitted to the works, except on business.

WHEN DID THE MURDER TAKE PLACE?

Other workmen who have been interviewed on the subject say it was impossible that the remains could have been in the place where they were found more than two or three days. They know for a fact that it was not there last Friday. The medical opinion is that death was caused about a month ago, and that will correspond with the time at which the arm was found in the Thames at Pimlico. That was Sept. 11, and the arm was thought to have been in the water three days, which would make the date of the crime September 5th, the same day on which the woman Annie Chapman was murdered in Whitechapel. The arm has been preserved in spirits, so that no difficulty will be experienced in seeing if it forms portion of the same body. A careful examination of the remains is to be made by medical men this morning. The discovery caused great excitement in London last night when the public became aware of the circumstance, through late extra special editions of the evening papers.

THE WESTMINSTER DISCOVERY AND THE PIMLICO MYSTERY.

It is satisfactory to state, says the Central News, that in view of the possibility of a discovery such as that made yesterday, the arms found at Westminster and Lambeth a short time ago, of which mention is made below, were not buried, as had been supposed. They have been preserved in the usual way, and will be taken to the mortuary in which the trunk now lies. One of the first things which the surgeons will have to do to-day will be to test by actual experiment whether the discovered limbs belong to the trunk found yesterday, and the result will be awaited with profound interest and anxiety, for if they do not fit the trunk we shall be driven to the conclusion that not one, but two more mysterious and horrible crimes have been committed in our midst. For the present the police and surgical experts are hopeful that the various fragments will be found to be part of the same body. Even then much will remain to be discovered. The head, the most important part for purposes of identification, and the legs are still missing. As to the remaining limbs the only thing certain is that two arms have been found. The first arm was found on the afternoon of September 11th by a man named Moore, who works in a timber yard in Grosvenor Road, Westminster. The palms and the tapering fingers indicated that the victim had belonged to the middle or possibly even the upper grade of society. In the opinion of the surgeons who examined the limb, although the knife had been adroitly used, it was not wielded by a surgical expert, and it had certainly never been inside a dissecting room. Everything, in fact, seemed to point to murder, and with this view, it is understood, the police reluctantly agreed, and orders were given for the river to be dragged; and every effort was made for the detection of the murderer should he endeavour, as it was reasonable to suppose, to dispose of the other parts of his victim's body. Nothing occurred, however, until the 19th ultimo, when a second arm was found in Southwark. A boy was walking along the Lambeth Road about half-past seven o'clock on the morning of that date when he noticed, just within the Blind School Garden, a parcel which curiosity prompted him to inspect more closely. He reached it, opened it, and saw to his horror that it enclosed a human arm. The limb was somewhat decomposed, and lime had been thrown over it, but it was recognisable as that of a woman. It was handed over to the police of the L Division, and after that came into their possession little more was heard of it, the police maintaining the utmost reserve regarding the discovery. In fact the police all denied any knowledge of a human arm having been found, but the boy above mentioned - who is a shoeblack - adhered to his statement that the limb was removed to Kennington Lane Police Station. The boy's statement was in some measure confirmed by that of Jim Moore, a bricklayer, who stated that he saw the boy pick up the parcel, and that he himself saw the arm. The boy, on being further questioned, said the parcel had attracted the notice of others before he passed, but that he was the first to open it.

THEORIES AS TO THE MYSTERY.

Persons who had seen the trunk describe it as being in a particularly advanced stage of decomposition, so much so that it was pronounced dangerous by the medical gentlemen present for any one to touch it with the naked hand. An extraordinary fact is that the lower portion of the trunk from the ribs has been removed. It is pronounced by the medical gentlemen to have belonged to a remarkably fine young woman. Has the Pimlico mystery then any connection with the series of murders which have been perpetrated in Whitechapel? This question naturally occurs when it is known that certain portions of the abdomen are missing, but there is also another theory equally well founded. It is that the young woman, of whose body portions are now coming to light in such a mysterious manner, has been the victim of an unlawful operation, and in order to conceal this the miscreant has removed that portion of the body which would almost undoubtedly have decided such a point.

Western Times - Thursday 04 October 1888

THE WHITEHALL MYSTERY.

London, Wednesday Evening. The surgeons who conducted the autopsy on the remains found at Westminster, came to the conclusion that the arm which was washed up by the Thames near Pimlico, and which had been conveyed to Westminster mortuary from Ebary-street, where it had been preserved, fitted into the trunk found at Whitehall. It is also stated that the cord tied round the limb found in the river, and a portion of that which was used to tie the parcel, were similar. At the conclusion of the examination the clothing was disinfected and thoroughly inspected by the police. Adhering to one portion was found a piece of newspaper saturated with blood. It bore no date, but that can easily be ascertained. The dress stuff was found to be a rich flowered silk underskirt, which proves that the unfortunate victim was not one of the poorer class of Society. Nothing was discovered to indicate the cause of death, but the doctors are of opinion that the woman had been murdered about three weeks, and the advanced stage decomposition was due to exposure. The doctors are preparing an elaborate report on the whole case which will be submitted at the inquest to be held on Monday next.

Edinburgh Evening News - Thursday 04 October 1888

THE WHITEHALL MYSTERY.

The Press Association says an inspector and a number of plain-clothes police were again searching the basement of the new police offices in Whitehall this morning for the remaining members of the body found there on Tuesday. It is believed the person who deposited the remains was familiar with the ground, the passages leading to the spot being dark and full of pitfalls.

Sheffield Evening Telegraph - Friday 05 October 1888

THE WHITEHALL MYSTERY.
ALLEGED IMPORTANT EVIDENCE.

The Press Association says that Detective Inspector Marshall, of the Whitehall Police, this morning proceeded to Guildford to obtain some human remains, consisting principally of the leg of a woman which were picked up on the railway there some time ago. Dr. Bond will then compare them with the trunk lying at the Westminster Mortuary. It is currently stated among the police that some important evidence has been obtained that may lead to the identification of the body, and probably to an arrest.

South Wales Daily News - Saturday 06 October 1888

A MAN WITH A MYSTERIOUS PARCEL.
THE DISCOVERY OF A HUMAN LEG AT GUILDFORD.

Some sensation was caused in Guildford yesterday by the report that the remains which were discovered on August 24th in a brown paper parcel lying on the railway near the station were supposed to be part of the body of the woman the trunk of which was found in a vault of the new police barracks at Whitehall. It will be remembered that the remains found at Guildford consisted of a right foot and portion of a left leg from the knee down to the ankle, where it bad been severed. The police doctor examined the limbs at the time, and certified them to be human, while he also considered them to be those of a woman, but the flesh bad been either roasted or boiled. No clue had been found to solve the mystery, but after the discovery at Whitehall, Supt. Barry, of the Guildford borough police, wrote to the Scotland Yard authorities, with the result that Detective- Inspector Marshall, who has the Whitehall mystery in hand, proceeded yesterday to Guildford, and had the remains, which had been buried in the cemetery, disinterred, and in the evening he conveyed them to London. Mr Marshall, in reply to our correspondent, stated that he could form no opinion as to whether the remains were part of the trunk, but he would immediately take them to Dr Bond and Dr Hibberd, by whom they would be carefully examined. Detective-Inspector Marshall, assisted by a number of colleagues, is also pursuing the search for a clue in another direction, and as already stated, difficult as the task seems, they by no means despair of establishing the identity of the deceased woman. Since the publication of the fact of the finding of the body quite a number of persons have been in communication with the police both with reference to missing friends, whom they thought more or less answered the description of the victim, and to communicate suspicious circumstances which they had observed leading them now to suspect that a crime has been perpetrated. Every instance of the kind is being thoroughly investigated under the direction of Chief Superintendent Dunlop and Chief Inspector Wren, of the A Division. There does not now seem much doubt but that the maker of the skirt will ultimately be found, whilst there are two other possible clues which the police are also working upon, but of which it is not advisable to give the details at present. Dr Bond and his colleague are inclined to place the possibility of the woman's death as having occurred so long ago as August last, somewhere about the 24th of that month. Owing to the condition in which the body was at the period of its discovery, this date is, of course, more or less conjectural.

A *Star* reporter had an interview yesterday with Mr Edward Deuchar, who has communicated some important information to the police which may assist in the discovery of the man who deposited the body in Whitehall. Mr Deuchar, a little over three weeks ago, went on a tramcar from Vauxhall Station to London Bridge. He noticed a man on the car carrying a parcel. He would not have taken particular notice of the parcel but for the fact that there was a terrible smell emanating from it. The olfactory organs of most of the passengers were affected by the extraordinary stench, which pervaded all the car. The parcel seemed to be heavy, and the man carried it with extreme care under his arm. It was tied up in brown paper. The top of it was under his arm, while he held the corner end in his hand. Mr Deuchar says the man looked ill at ease and agitated. He described him as a powerfully built man, of rough appearance, with a goatee beard. He was rather shabbily dressed.

Lloyd's Weekly Newspaper - Sunday 07 October 1888

THE WHITEHALL MYSTERY.

As yet the police have not been able to trace the identity of the female whose mutilated trunk was found on the site of the new police headquarters on the Thames embankment at Whitehall on Tuesday. On Friday Detective-inspector Marshall proceeded to Guildford to bring to London some remains discovered near the railway line there on Aug. 24 in a brown paper parcel, thinking they might belong to those found in London. Yesterday when the remains arrived in London, however, it was found that they were not human at all, but those of some animal.

The parts discovered at Whitehall have been lying in a disinfectant bath, but are now taken out to be dried, and reduced as far as possible to the natural size and shape. It is understood that the hands and the fingers are of long and delicate construction on the right arm that was lately recovered. The police are searching in all directions for the missing portions of the body - namely, the head; the lower part of the trunk, the left arm, the two legs and feet. The head, of course, the authorities are most anxious to find; and the Thames will be closely watched and dragged.

With reference to any clue, the police state that they have very little at present. Since the publication of the shocking discovery they had received up to yesterday over 500 applications and inquiries about missing friends. Dr. Bond and Dr. Hebbert made a further examination yesterday, but it is understood they cannot yet form a very definite opinion as to the age, size, and general complexion of the deceased.

As in former Thames mysteries, any new discovery will be awaited with great interest. It will be recollected that in the case of the Richmond murder the head of Mrs. Thomas was never found. Kate Webster was entreated to say what she had done with it, and it is asserted that she kept the secret till just before she was executed, when she stated that she carefully dropped it between some supports of Old Battersea-bridge, down which it slid till it got to the bottom of the Thames. The secret was kept for several years, and we believe has never yet been published. It will be well, therefore, to search for any missing remains in this case in unsuspected nooks and corners.

Western Times - Monday 08 October 1888

THE WHITEHALL MYSTERY.

An examination of the remains brought to London from Guildford by Inspector Marshall was made on Saturday by Dr. Bond at Westminster Hospital, and it has been ascertained that they do not belong to the trunk discovered in tbe vault at Whitehall. In fact, the opinion of the medical man is that they are not human remains at all.

London, Sunday Night. The result of the examination by Drs. Bond and Hibberd of the remains which were brought frem Guildford revealed that they belonged to a bear. The trunk found at Whitehall and the arm discovered at Pimlico have been taken out of the spirits in which they were being preserved, in order to be dried and endeavour made to restore them to their normal size and shape. Instructions have also been given for them to be photographed tomorrow morning. At the inquest which will be opened to-morrow afternoon evidence will be given of the finding of the parcel and its removal by the police, after which the all-important medical testimony will be adduced. The inquiry will then probably be adjourned for a few weeks to await the result of further inquiries by the police.

Daily Gazette for Middlesbrough - Monday 08 October 1888

THE WHITEHALL MYSTERY.
MISSING YOUNG WOMEN.
EXTRAORDINARY STORY.

In connection with this mystery the detective [???] are most assiduously investigating cases of missing young women, and their attention has been specially directed to the remarkable disappearance of a girl named Lily Vass, between 16 and 17 years of age, who left her home, No. 45, Tetcott road, Chelsea on July 19 last, and has never been seen or heard of since. On the 27th October Mrs Vass, the mother of the young woman, applied to Mr Biron, the sitting magistrate at the Westminster Police Court, and some publicity was given to the extraordinary disappearance of her daughter, who was stated to be of rather prepossessing appearance. The detective police have several times called on Mrs

Vass to obtain additional particulars about the girl, and at their request the mother accompanied the an officer to the Millbank mortuary to view the remains there. She was, however, quite unequal to the ordeal of making an inspection, and only saw the black flowered satine skirt in which the body was found. She could not recognise this, and she was more disposed to discredit the supposition that the remains were those of her daughter from the fact that one of the police officers told her that the body belonged to a woman at least 25 years of age. In an interview a person had with Mrs Vass at her house on Friday night she gave many additional particulars as to the disappearance of her daughter. She said that her daughter was in service with a lady in Sealcott road, Wandsworth Common, and on the 19th of July she left home ostensibly to go back to her situation.

"Although I had always found her a truthful girl, I am bound to say she deceived me in one respect," said Mrs Vass. "She had left her situation, although she told me she had not. I think it was on the Monday she came home, and she left on the Thursday. She was seen wearing a black straw hat trimmed with crepe, and a very dark ulster with a velvet trimming front. She was a dark-complexioned girl, fairly stout, quite of medium height – 5ft. 5in. certainly and her dress was of black and white material – nothing like that I saw at the mortuary, but of course that goes for nothing. She had dark hair, fringed on the forehead, and her face was round and fresh coloured. We think she must have been enticed away. She was not a girl who kept a lot of company, and I believe the only person who ever wrote to her was a girl in service at Notting Hill. Lily has kept her places two or three years at a time, but she had only been with the old lady at Wandsworth about six months. If she is alive she must have been taken away right out of London, for we have looked and enquired everywhere for her, and can get no tidings." Questioned as to how the girl left home, the mother went on to say:- "She told me, as I have already said, that she was going back to her place at Wandsworth, and that she thought she was going to travel with her mistress to the Isle of Wight. She left behind her macintosh and bag, and went away with nothing but the clothes she stood upright in. I was not surprised at first, because she explained that she had left her box with a charwoman, of Chatham road, Wandsworth Common. Everything pointed to the belief that she was going back to service, because she promised to send her brother a shilling to spend 'at a treat,' and to repay me a very small sum I advanced her.

She was a girl not devoid of sense, but rather abrupt in manner. I think that if she were alive she would write, even if she did not wish me to know where she was. Interrogated as to the possible identity of her daughter with the victim of the mysterious crime now being investigated by the A Division detectives, Mrs Vass, somewhat distressed, said she hardly knew what to think – so many dreadful things were happening. Of course, recognition of the remains without the head was well-nigh impossible, and so much depended on what the doctor said. Her daughter had fine arms, and her hand was rough from hard work. The only marks along the girl's body were on the neck and they were the scars of old abscesses that were lanced.

The police do not disguise the fact that they have uncovered important information which will lead to the identification of the murdered woman, and possibly to the arrest of the perpetrator of the crime. One officer states that the maker of the silk skirt in which the body was found has been discovered. The maker is the proprietor of a West End establishment. Having discovered so much, it is probable the person who ordered and received the skirt will be reached. Thus some sensational development of the case is anticipated. The date of the committal of the crime was fixed under rather peculiar circumstances. The piece of a London paper adhering to the remains was only about six inches long and four broad. Upon searching the files at the office of the paper, however, it was found that it was a portion of an edition published on the 24th of August. The doctors and the police thereupon came to the conclusion, comparing this with the post-mortem indications, that the deed must have been committed either on that date or shortly anterior thereto.

Mr Edward Deuchar has communicated some information to the police which may afford a clue to the discovery of the man who deposited the body of the woman in Whitehall and the arm in the Thames. Mr Deuchar is a commercial traveller, and a little over three weeks ago he went on a tram-car from Vauxhall Station to London Bridge. It is stated that he noticed a man on the car carrying a parcel. He would not have taken particular notice of the parcel but for the fact that there was a terrible smell emanating from it. The olfactory organs of most of the passengers were affected by the extraordinary stench which pervaded the car. A lady gave her husband, who was sitting next to the man, some lavender to hold to his nose. The parcel seemed to be heavy. The man carried it with extreme care under his arm. It was tied up in brown paper. The top of it was under his arm, while he held the corner end in his hand. Mr Deuchar says the man looked ill at ease and agitated. He described him as a powerfully-built man, of rough appearance, and with a goatee beard, and rather shabbily dressed. Mr Deuchar is confident that he could recognise him again. The car went on, and when at the Obelisk, St. George's Circus, several persons alighted. Mr Deuchar still remained on the car, but when about thirty yards from the Obelisk, said: "This stench is awful; I can't stand it any longer," and proceeded to get out. Just at that moment the suspicious looking individual with the parcel asked the conductor, "Have we passed the Obelisk yet?" and then jumped out. Mr Deuchar, when he had descended and walked some distance towards London Bridge, called a policeman's attention to the retreating form of the "man with the stinking parcel," and told him to "keep an eye on him."

Sheffield Evening Telegraph - Monday 08 October 1888

THE WHITEHALL MYSTERY.
SCENES AT THE INQUEST TO-DAY.
JURORS VIEW THE BODY THROUGH A WINDOW.
A HORRIBLE SPECTACLE.

The inquest on the body of a woman who is the victim of the "Whitehall mystery" was held in London this afternoon, and the jury, before hearing the evidence, went to view the remains. The body in the mortuary presented an awful spectacle. It was locked in a room, and was viewed by the jury through a window, from fear of contagion. It was on a table propped up, and the arm recently found was placed in the socket. The body was of a dark brown colour. At 20 minutes past three the first witness was called.

FREDERICK WILDBORN CARPENTER, employed on the works. He said he first saw what he thought was an old [???] on Monday morning. He took no notice of the matter then, and saw the parcel again the same evening. On the following day he called the assistant foreman's attention to the parcel. It was then found to contain the body of a woman. He did not notice any smell. Witness pointed out the spot where the body was found on a maze-like plan of the vaults, and he said it would be very difficult for any one unacquainted with the place to find his way there. The workmen's tools had been placed there for ten weeks up to two weeks before the body was found.

GEO. BUDGEY, bricklayer's labourer, engaged in the works, said he was told by another workman to go and see what the parcel was. He untied the parcel, and produced the cord which had served that purpose. The body was then seen, and the police were sent for.

Detective THOMAS HAWKINS, A Division, deposed to being called and seeing the body. It was wrapped in [???] material (produced). The wall was very black, and the body was in a very advanced stage of decomposition. The vaults were very dark, and no stranger could have found his way without a light. The person would have to cross a trench which could not be seen in the dark.

FREDERICK MOORE deposed to finding the arm lying in the Mortuary. The arm was not wrapped up, but a piece of string was tied tightly around the top of the arm.

WILLIAM JAMES, 127 B, said he was called to where the arm was found. He took it to the police station, and called Dr. Meville. The arm was subsequently taken to Ebury Bridge Mortuary.

CHARLES WM. BROWN, assistant foreman to Messrs. Grover, the contractors for the works, said the vaults had been completed three months. There was no watchman at night, but the three doors were locked. Strangers would not have known that such a place existed. Witness did not notice on Monday that the locks to the gates had been tampered with.

GEORGE CHIN, the foreman, deposed to being called to see the body.

EARNEST HEAD said he was in the vault on the Saturday before the Tuesday when the body was found. He had a paraffin lamp, but saw no parcel.

York Herald - Monday 08 October 1888

IMPORTANT DISCOVERIES.

London, Saturday, Noon. - Respecting the Westminster mystery, it is to-day stated that the police have discovered that the flowered skirt round the corpse was obtained from a London West-End draper, and that the piece of newspaper wrapped up with the body belongs to one bearing date August 24th, which is further said to be the date on which the remains were found at Guildford.

THE GUILDFORD "MYSTERY."

Last night, the result of the examination by Doctors Bond and Hibberd of the remains which were brought from Guildford revealed that they belonged to a bear. The trunk found at White-hall, and arms discovered at Pimlico, have been taken out of the spirit in which they were being preserved in order to be buried, and an endeavour made to restore them to their normal size and shape. Instructions have also been given for them to be photographed.

Manchester Courier and Lancashire General Advertiser - Monday 08 October 1888

FROM OUR LONDON CORRESPONDENT

London, Sunday Night. At the time of writing I do not know whether the police have made a capture in connection with what is known as the Whitehall mystery. But for the fact that it has been overshadowed by the crime at the other end of London the mystery would have caused a commotion in the metropolis, the like of which has not been witnessed since the discovery of the remains of Harriet Lane. If the police are not on the wrong scent they will trace the murder of the woman, whose mutilated remains have been found in different places, to a person occupying a much higher position in the social sphere than did Wainwright. Rumour at times like these invariably gets in advance of truth, but in what are known as Government circles, and in other places where men are well informed, highly sensational revelations are anticipated.

Western Daily Press - Tuesday 09 October 1888

THE WHITEHALL MYSTERY.
THE INQUEST: IMPORTANT MEDICAL EVIDENCE.

Mr Troutbeck, coroner for Westminster, yesterday afternoon opened an inquest on the remains of a woman discovered under the new police offices on the Thames Embankment last Monday. The remains consisted of the trunk and an arm, the latter having been previously found at Pimlico.

Frederick Wildborn, a carpenter, employed at the works, who found the trunk, said the place where it was secreted in the vaults was very difficult of access to anyone unacquainted with the building.

Detective Thomas Hawkings, of the A Division, deposed to being called to see the body. He produced some dress material in which it was wrapped. He described the vaults as very dark, and difficult for a stranger to find his way without a light. A person would have to cross a trench, which could not be seen in the darkness.

Frederick Moore deposed to finding the arm, which was in the mortuary. The arm was not wrapped up, but a piece of string was tied tightly round the top of it.

Police-Constable William James, 127B, said he was called to where the arm was found, at Grosvenor Road, Pimlico. He took it to the police station, and called Dr. Neville. The arm was subsequently taken to the mortuary at Ebury Bridge.

Charles William Brown, assistant foreman to Messrs Grover, the contractors for the works at Whitehall, said the vaults had been completed three months. There was no watchman at night, but the three doors were locked. A stranger would not know that such a place existed. Witness did not notice on Monday that locks to the gates had been tampered with.

George Chin, the foreman, deposed to being called to see the remains.

Ernest Head said he was in the vault on the Saturday prior to discovery. He had a paraffin lamp, but saw no parcel.

Dr. Bond said that on the day the body was found he was called to see it. It was that of a woman, and was very much decomposed, causing the wall where body had been to be quite discoloured. The head had been sawn from the trunk, the pelvis and lower part of the abdomen also being separated by the same instrument. The body was well nourished. The chest measured thirty-five and a half inches, and the waist twenty-eight and a half inches. The breasts were well formed, and gave evidence of the woman not having had a child. The arms had been removed by several downward incisions, which were skilfully done. The lungs showed that the woman had at some time suffered from pleurisy, and from other indications it was ascertained that she had not been drowned or suffocated. The woman had a fair skin and dark hair. The body had been dead about two months, and had decomposed in the air and not water. The parts missing from the victims of the recent Whitechapel murders were also absent from the trunk. He subsequently examined the arm found in the Thames, off Pimlico, on the 11th of September. It accurately fitted the trunk, the cuts and the general contour of the arm corresponding to those of the body. It was quite possible that the woman had had a child, but the indications were against that supposition. There was nothing to show the actual cause of death, but he was of opinion that it was from loss of blood. The witness said that the deceased appeared to have been a woman of about 24 or 25 years of age. She seemed to have been large, well nourished, of fair skin, and dark hair. The appearance of the breast rather indicated that she had not suckled a child.

The Coroner: She might have had a child?

Witness: Yes.

The Coroner: She appeared to have been dead six weeks or two months. The decomposition occurred in the air, not the water.

Do you see the arm which has been spoken of? - Yes, I found the arm accurately fitted to the trunk. The arm was that of a woman. The hand was large, the fingers tapering, and the nails well shaped. It was quite the hand of a person not used to manual labour.

Were the cuts made after death? - Undoubtedly, but it was impossible, owing to the state of decomposition about the neck, to say whether a cut had been made there during life.

So that there was nothing to indicate the cause of death? - No.

Was it a sudden death? - l cannot say, except that death was not from drowning or suffocation, but was more likely from hemorrhage or fainting.

Can you say anything as to the height of the woman? - We believe the height to have been about 5 feet 5 inches.

Was she very stout? - Not very stout, but thoroughly plump; no abnormal excess of fat.

Did the hand show any sign of refinement? - l don't know that a hand of that kind is always associated with refinement of mind or body, but certainly it was a refined hand.

Dr. Hibbert, assistant to the last witness, said he had examined the arm referred to. It had been separated from the body after death. The cut in the skin and bone exactly corresponded to the trunk. A certain amount of skill was shown in severing the limbs and in tying the parcel, but not the skill of the dissecting room.

Inspector Marshall, who has charge of the case, said the piece of dress in which the body was wrapped was of broche satin cloth, of Bradford manufacture, but of an old pattern - probably three years ago. It was a rather common material, costing about sixpence-half-penny a yard when new. There was a six-inch flounce at the bottom of the dress.

At this point the inquiry was adjourned for a fortnight

Sheffield Independent - Thursday 11 October 1888

THE WHITEHALL MYSTERY.

Since the inquest on Monday, Inspector Marshall has been diligently prosecuting inquiries in connection with the finding of the trunk of a woman at Whitehall, and it is expected that he will be in a position to furnish farther important evidence at the adjourned inquest on the 22nd inst. The spot where the body was found is still watched by the police, who will continue to guard the place until after the inquest. The fact that every one is of opinion that no stranger could have put the parcel in such an out-of-the-way corner considerably narrows the inquiry, and on Monday week other workmen will be called, who will prove that the parcel was not in the vault on the Saturday before the Monday when it was found. The men engaged on the works have taken the matter in hand, and are endeavouring to ascertain the person who is responsible for depositing the remains in the vault, and no stone is being left unturned to discover some clue to the mystery.

Illustrated Police News - Saturday 13 October 1888

DISCOVERING THE MUTILATED TRUNK

MILLBANK STREET MORTUARY.

Aberdeen Evening Express - Tuesday 16 October 1888

The Detective Department have been engaged inquiring into a story told by a person living at Llanelly regarding the Whitehall mystery, to the effect that two men brought a full sack on a truck to a hoarding round the building where the body was found, while a third man climbed over to aid in hiding the sack. The incident has been conclusively proved to have had nothing to do with the mystery. Three men had brought a bag of sand, and one got over to open the door for the others.

Hull Daily Mail - Wednesday 17 October 1888

THE LONDON MURDERS.
THE WHITEHALL MYSTERY.
FURTHER REMAINS FOUND.

The place where the trunk of the woman was found in the new police buildings, at Whitehall, was further examined this morning, when a Spitzbergen belonging to Mr Jasper T. C. Waring was employed. The dog began to sniff at the mound of earth, which was dug over, and when much of the soil had been removed the dog seized a strange looking object, which on being examined by a candle was found to be a portion of a human leg which had been severed at the knee-joint. Upon the leg was a portion of a stocking of some woollen substance. It is remarkable that the leg was found only a yard and a half from the spot where the body was found, and the police were supposed to have searched the whole of the ground. A medical man was summoned, and he at once took charge of the limb with a view of making a detailed examination of it.

Dundee Courier - Thursday 18 October 1888

THE WHITEHALL MYSTERY.
DISCOVERY OF MORE HUMAN REMAINS.

Yesterday morning a further discovery of human remains was made on the site of the Police Buildings in Whitehall. Mr Jasper Waring having obtained permission of the police and the contractor to use a Spitzbergen dog, the animal was taken into a vault where the trunk of a woman was discovered a fortnight ago, and in a short time it began sniffing at a mound of earth which had been thrown back from an excavation for a drain made eight or ten weeks ago. A labourer, who was with the search party, was at once directed to throw over some of the soil, and about a foot from the surface an object was found, which was at once seized upon by the dog. Examination proved it to be a portion of a human leg, in which decomposition was far advanced. The limb when found was lying eight or nine feet from the spot where the woman's trunk was discovered. The constable on duty at the works sent information of the discovery to King Street Police Station, ordering that the digging should in the meantime be discontinued. Officers of the Criminal Investigation Department quickly arrived, and Dr Bond, who was one of the surgeons who made the post mortem examination of the trunk, was summoned. He pronounced the limb to be that of a finely developed woman. It was the left leg, and had been severed at the knee, and the doctor's opinion was that it had been in the vault for about six weeks. The limb was afterward conveyed to the mortuary. During the last fortnight a strict guard has been kept over the works by the police, and access to the premises could not have been attempted within that time without certainty of detection. Digging was afterwards resumed up to half-past four yesterday afternoon, when the the search was discontinued for the day, but no further discovery was made.

The discovery was made by a dog of a somewhat mongrel breed, belonging to a gentleman whose faith in its scenting powers induced him to offer its services to the police. The dog was taken to the vault, and almost immediately led the small party of searchers to a small pile of loose and broken bricks. The soil was turned up to a depth of about six inches, and a human leg and foot, much decomposed, was found. The remains had evidently lain when found for at least six weeks, and it is, to say the least, extraordinary that they were not discovered at the time the police were supposed to have made a thorough search a fortnight ago. Dr Bond, who made the post mortem examination of the trunk, was quickly summoned to the spot, and ordered the removal of the leg to the mortuary. To-day he will make an examination with a view to settle the question whether the leg fits the trunk, but of this it is understood there is practically no doubt. The arm found at Westminster is still at the mortuary, and it is hoped that sooner or later the remaining portions of the body, and especially the head, will be brought together. It is now thought that the woman was actually murdered in the vaults below the new police offices, and that most of the limbs were hidden there. The police have decided to undertake another “thorough” search.

South Wales Daily News - Thursday 18 October 1888

Alter a period of comparative quietude, the streets are alive again to-night with cries of "Extra Special," and "Discovery or Fresh Human Remains." These turn out to be a leg and a foot unearthed at Whitehall, not far from the place where the trunk of a woman was recently found. It is believed by the authorities that these are portions of the body on which an inquest was held a short time ago. The police are much more sanguine of success in tracing out this Whitehall mystery than they are of coming on the track of the Whitechapel murderer. In the latter case there is absolutely no clue. In the former it is evident that a woman, brought up in respectable, if not affluent circumstances, has come to her death, and that some person or persons nearly concerned in the transaction have been at great pains secretly to make away with the body. Enquiries are being made in every direction with the object of ascertaining whether any woman answering to the general description evolved by consideration of the trunk found at Whitehall has within the past month or six weeks disappeared from home or from her usual haunts.

Shields Daily Gazette - Thursday 18 October 1888

THE WHITEHALL MYSTERY.
THE REMAINS EXAMINED.

The Press Association says that, contrary to expectation, the search at the new police office buildings in

Whitechapel was resumed late last night by means of candles. A bloodhound, one of those which had been used in the Hyde Park experiment, was brought from the King Street police station, and a staff of constables, with Inspectors Peters and Marshall, were engaged for an hour and a half in turning over the earth, but no new discovery was made. Dr Bond, Divisional Surgeon, made an examination this morning of the portion of the leg found yesterday, and, on comparing it with the trunk already in the mortuary, he is of opinion that it is a portion of the same body, but much better preserved, the reason for this being that it was sufficiently buried to exclude the air. Dr Bond also believes both portions found have been lying in the place for over six weeks.

South Wales Daily News - Friday 19 October 1888

THE WHITEHALL MYSTERY.
EXAMINATION OF THE LIMB.

It has transpired that some time ago a carman saw two men and a boy with a cart conveying a large bundle stop outside the works. The boy scaled the hoarding, and opened the wicket-gate, through which the men carried the bundle.

Contrary to expectation, the search at the new police-office buildings in Whitehall was resumed on Wednesday night by means of candles. A bloodhound, one of those which had been used in the Hyde Park experiment, was brought from King-street police-station and a staff of constables, with Inspectors Peters and

Marshall, were engaged for an hour a half in turning over the earth; but on work being suspended at 10 p.m. no new discovery had been made. The search was resumed on Thursday forenoon, when the hound was again taken to the spot.

Dr Bond, the divisional surgeon, made an examination on Thursday of the portion of the leg found the previous day, and on comparing it with the trunk already in the mortuary, is of opinion that it is a portion of the same body, but much better preserved. The reason for this being that it was sufficiently buried to escape the air. Dr Bond also believes portions found have been lying in the place for over six weeks. The examination lasted for some time, but no marks which might lead to identification were discernible. The foot and leg are exquisitely moulded and the foot has been well cared for the nails being well trimmed, while the corns of bunions, which would probably distinguish a poor woman, are absent. It is stated that the police are going to pump out the well at the new police buildings, and that it will be thoroughly searched for further remains.

Morning Post - Friday 19 October 1888

THE WHITEHALL MYSTERY.

The search at the new police buildings in Whitehall, which on Wednesday night proved unsuccessful as far as the discovery of more human remains was concerned, was not continued yesterday. The pumping out of the well on the premises, however, was continued, but, so far, it has not been attended with any important results. Mr. Bond, divisional surgeon, made a careful examination yesterday morning, at Millbank-street, of a portion of the leg which was found on the previous day, and, on comparing it with the trunk already in the mortuary, he is of opinion that it belongs to the same body. It is, however, in a better state of preservation, and this is accounted for by the fact that it had been sufficiently covered with earth to exclude the air, whereas the trunk was only wrapped up in a skirt. Mr. Bond is also of opinion that both portions of the body had been lying where they were found for over six weeks, not-withstanding the statement made by people at the works that they were not there on the Friday or Saturday previous to their discovery. The examination lasted for some time, but no marks which might lead to identification were discernible.

Yorkshire Post and Leeds Intelligencer - Saturday 20 October 1888

THE WHITEHALL MYSTERY.

The opinion is largely entertained in official circles that the remainder of the body, portions of which have already been discovered, is somewhere in the vault beneath the site of the new police buildings. Further experiments are to be made with bloodhounds and other dogs. The opinion expressed by the medical men with regard to the remains so far discovered is that they belong to a young woman in an eminently high social position in life. It is thought that should the mystery ever be unravelled the disclosures will constitute a very sensational chapter of criminal history.

Illustrated Police News - Saturday 20 October 1888

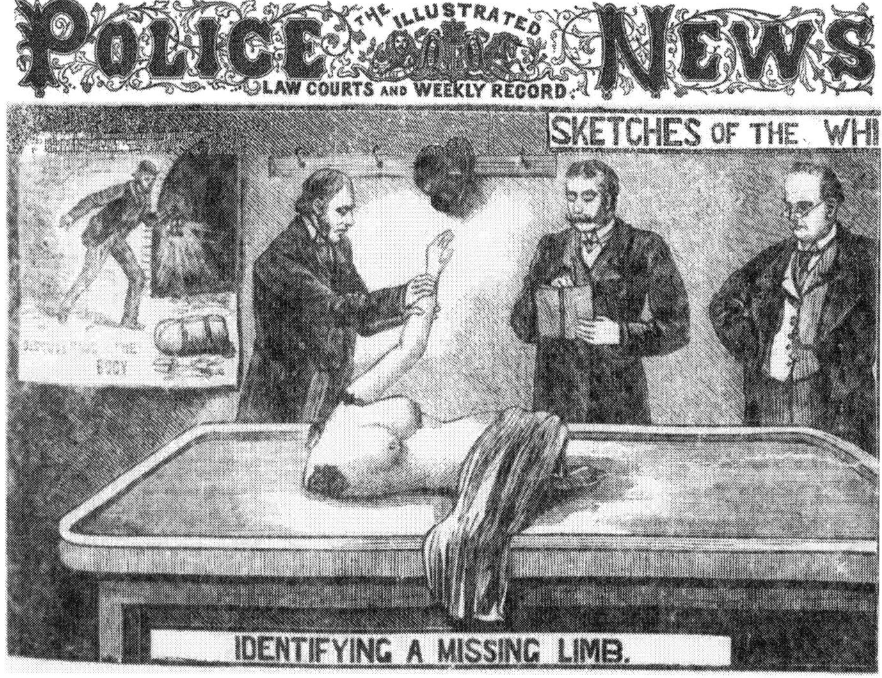

St James's Gazette - Tuesday 23 October 1888

The inquest upon the unfortunate creature whose mangled remains have been discovered partly in the vaults of the new police-buildings at Whitehall and partly in the river, is very inconclusive indeed. It leaves the matter, as it was to be feared it would, exactly where it was. There is nothing to show the identity of the victim - nothing to suggest when, where, or how she was murdered, no indication of the murderer or of the means by which the body was concealed in the vaults. Everything about the crime is as mysterious as it can be; and the remains had even lain unsuspected at Whitehall for weeks. There is every reason to fear that this must be added to the list of crimes unaccounted for, and perhaps unaccountable.

St James's Gazette - Tuesday 23 October 1888

THE WHITEHALL MYSTERY.
INQUEST AND VERDICT.

The adjourned inquest on the remains recently discovered in a vault of the new police buildings at Whitehall was resumed at the Sessions House, Westminster, yesterday afternoon, before Mr. Troutbeck, the coroner. The first witness was Mr. Brown, the deputy foreman of the works. He said he was of opinion that the trunk discovered on the 2nd of October could not have been in the position in which it was found on the 28th of September. The witness was then occupied in measuring the vault for the surveyor. No watchman had been employed on the works on the Saturday - that is to say, Saturday was the watchman's day off. Plans of the vault and superstructures were produced by the witness. George Erant, clerk of works, deposed that he left the building at midday on Saturdays. On the Friday preceding the discovery he was in the vault, but saw nothing of the body. He must have noticed it had it been there.

Richard Lawrence, labourer, said that on the Saturday prior to the discovery he was in the vault and left his tools there. He saw nothing of the remains. It was very dark. On Monday morning at six o'clock he went to the vault to fetch the tools, and, as on the previous occasion, he saw nothing to arouse his suspicions. Alfred Young, labourer, said he was in the vault on Saturday and saw nothing. It was very dark, however, and the body might have been there without his perceiving it. Arthur Franklin, surveyor, stated that he was in the vault on the Friday taking measurements. He saw nothing beyond a quantity of rubbish, but the body might have been there without attracting his attention.

Jasper Waring, who refused to give his address publicly and described himself as the Tilbury representative of a news-agency, said that he visited the site of the police-buildings in Whitehall with a dog on the 17th inst. He gave a detailed description of the discovery - the particulars of which have been already published - of a woman's leg through the agency of his dog. In reply to a juryman, the witness said he did not have permission of the police to visit the ground. Mr. Angle, a journalist, who accompanied Mr. Waring, gave corroborative evidence. J. Hedges, a labourer, said he was the last person in the vault on the Saturday in question. He went there for a hammer. He looked into the corner where the remains were unearthed, but saw nothing.

Dr. Bond said that he was called on the 17th inst, by Sergeant Rose, to Whitehall, where he found a leg and foot which he judged had been in the vault for several weeks. The foot was in an advanced stage of decomposition, but the leg was in wonderful state of preservation. The leg had been very cleverly disarticulated, and corresponded in every way with the trunk which he had previously examined. He had no doubt that the witness Hedges was quite wrong in what he said, and he was certain that the body had lain in the vault for weeks uncovered and exposed to the air. The brickwork was saturated with the decomposing fluid from a human body. Death in his opinion must have taken place about the end of August.

Mr. Hebbert of St. Thomas's Hospital, gave anatomical particulars of the leg discovered on the 17th inst. He bore out Dr. Bond's evidence. He thought the limb must have belonged to a woman of from 5 ft. 8 in. to 5 ft. 9 in. in height. He thought that death must have taken place about the middle of August.

Police-constable 363 A, and Sergeant Rose having given evidence, the coroner summed up very briefly. He said there was no evidence of identity beyond the fact established by the medical evidence - namely, that the remains were those of a well-developed female unaccustomed to manual labour. How the deceased came by her death there was no medical evidence to show; but all the evidence pointed to the probability of a violent death. The body had been mutilated after death, and this also was strong presumptive evidence of crime.

The jury returned a verdict of Found dead.

Shields Daily Gazette - Wednesday 31 October 1888

THE WHITEHALL MYSTERY.

Yesterday, the remains of the unknown female that were found recently at Whitehall were interred at Woking by the parish authorities, the order for burial having been handed over by Inspector Marshall, who has charge of the case. The remains, consisting of the trunk, arm, and leg, were removed from the mortuary in Millbank Street, Westminster, where they have lying to await identification, to Wallis's Yard Workhouse, and placed in a coffin, before being conveyed to their final resting place. Among the persons who called at the mortuary was an old woman who thought she recognised in the photograph which had been taken of the remains some trace of a daughter who had been missing since August, but she could not be positive upon the point.

CASE 3
Elizabeth Jackson
June 1889

Gloucester Citizen - Tuesday 04 June 1889

HORRIBLE DISCOVERY IN THE THAMES. ANOTHER HIDEOUS CRIME.

Two men named Regan and Kelly found a parcel by the side of the river Thames near St. George's stairs, Horselydown, which was found to contain the lower half of a woman's body which had been cut in half. The remains which bore no signs of decomposition, were wrapped in an apron. Information was at once given to the Thames police, who took charge of the remains, and will, no doubt, make inquiry with a view of finding the other parts.

London Evening Standard - Wednesday 05 June 1889

HORRIBLE DISCOVERT IN THE THAMES.

Parts of the mutilated body of a young woman were yesterday found in the Thames. From their condition it is evident that the remains had been in the water only a short time, and it is believed that the woman was murdered and that her body was cut up and thrown into the river. Yesterday morning three lads, whilst bathing near the Albert Bridge, Battersea Park, noticed a curious-looking object which the tide kept moving against the muddy foreshore. The lads went to the spot, and found that it was a human limb, partly covered by a white cloth. They dressed as quickly as possible, and wrapping the limb up as well as they could, they conveyed it to the nearest police-station. There it was found to be a woman's limb, from the hip joint to the knee, about sixteen inches long. The limb had been roughly and unskilfully severed from the trunk when the underclothing was still upon the body, and part of the linen remained. Upon it was written in marking ink, "L. E. Fisher." Fastened to the linen was a piece of black and grey check tweed, which had apparently belonged to a woman's ulster. It had been torn or roughly cut off. The police communicated with Scotland-yard, and the Assistant Divisional Surgeon for Battersea, Dr. Kempster, on seeing the limb, declared that it had not been in the water more than twenty-four hours. There were signs that previous to death the limb had been severely bruised. Everything seemed to show that the limb was that of a fair young woman of medium height, between twenty and twenty-five years of age.

Inspector John Tunbridge, and other officers of the Criminal Investigation Department, had scarcely had time to commence their investigations into this discovery, when news reached Scotland-yard that other human remains had been found at St. George's Stairs, Horselydown, a spot below London Bridge about five miles from the scene of the first discovery. John Regan, a labourer, was standing on the river bank, when he noticed some boys pelting a parcel, which bad been left by the tide just out of the water. Regan went to the object, and on untying the parcel found that it contained part of a body, which he handed to the Thames Police, who conveyed it to Wapping Police-station. This intelligence was sent to Scotland-yard, and Dr. Bond, Chief Surgeon to the Metropolitan Police, with several detective officers, proceeded to Wapping. Dr. Bond saw that the remains were those of a young woman, upon whom had been performed an unlawful operation. They consisted of the lower part of a female body, including the abdomen and the uterus, which had been part of a living body probably 24 hours previously, for blood was still flowing from the ragged edges where the knife or hatchet had been used. The parcel was conveyed to the nearest mortuary, where it was photographed. Dr. Bond who saw the limb found at Battersea had no doubt that it belonged to the same body as did the remains found at Horselydown. Part of the same undergarment which was found on the limb at Battersea was found in the parcel discovered at Horselydown. Everything tends to show that the operation, the death, and the dismemberment occurred within the space of a few hours.

Another account says: - A careful examination of the contents of the bundle found at Horselydown satisfied the doctors that they were portions of a body to which the leg discovered at Battersea belonged. This limb had been wrapped up in the corresponding half-piece of the pair of drawers to that used for enveloping the abdominal organs; and what is regarded as a valuable clue was furnished by the linen, which was marked “L. E. Fisher.” Whether this is the name of the dead woman or not the police are, of course, trying to ascertain, and are pursuing inquiries with the object of discovering whether a woman of that name has been missing from her friends within the last few weeks or days. In the opinion of the doctors, the woman had been dead only forty-eight hours, and the body had been dissected somewhat roughly by a person who, nevertheless, must have had some knowledge of the points of the human body. Appearances tend to prove that the woman quite recently had been delivered of a child, and there is some ground for the surmise that an unlawful operation in connection with this might have led to her death, to avert the discovery of which the body was cut up and thrown into the river. The woman was apparently about 25 years of age, 5ft. 6in. in height, and with bright auburn hair. Judging from all appearances, the police incline to the belief that the woman met her death by foul means. Of course in such cases suspicion is attached by some persons to the medical schools, but there is little evidence in the present case to support the idea that a practical joke has been carried out. Instructions have been issued for the most careful searching of the banks of the river, so as to bring to light, if possible, the missing parts of the body. Some of the riverside watermen are of opinion that the parcels were probably thrown into the river near Vauxhall or Battersea early yesterday morning.

Up till a late hour last night no further portions of the body had been discovered. Bargemen, watermen, and others employed on or about the river have been advised to keep a sharp look out, and to report to the police if they discover anything. Arrangements are also being made for a search of the river. It is considered probable that the main part of the body was buried, as in the case of the human trunk found at the new police office last year, and the search, therefore, will not be confined to the river.

Cambridge Daily News - Wednesday 05 June 1889

ANOTHER THAMES MYSTERY.
SUPPOSED MURDER OF WOMAN.
DISCOVER OF MUTILATED REMAINS.

Early on Tuesday morning, and almost simultaneously, two packages containing portions of a woman's mutilated body were discovered on the foreshore of the river Thames. Almost exactly at half-past ten o'clock the attention of a man named John Albert Kogan, a stevedore, was called by some children playing on the river bank at Horseleydown to a parcel which was floating in the water. He at once proceeded to get it out, the task not being one of much difficulty on account of the ebb tide, and the consequent shallow state of the water. By this time some other riverside workmen had been attracted to the spot, and they at once commenced to undo the parcel. They were horrified to discover that it contained the lower part of a woman's abdomen cut in two pieces, which had apparently been in the water only a comparatively short time. The remains were rather loosely wrapped up in one leg of a pair of woman's drawers, the band of the garment being used to fasten the parcel. A boat containing some Thames policemen happened to be passing at the time of the discovery, and the remains being handed over to them were conveyed with all speed to the river-side station at Wapping. The scene of this discovery is just opposite Cole's Upper Wharf, which abuts on Thomas-street, Tooley-street, Southwark, and it is evident from a cursory glance that the parcel did not get into the river in this district. Whilst this ghastly bundle was being examined news was received that another portion of a woman's body had been picked up from the Surrey side of the river, just by the Albert Bridge. In this case the parcel contained the left leg and thigh of a woman, who apparently in life was of good physical proportions. Dr. Bond (of Westminster Hospital) had the limb handed over to him for examination, and the authorities proceeded at once to endeavour to ascertain whether the two parcels had a common origin. Detective-inspector John Regan (detective-inspector of the Thames division) and Detective-inspector Tunbridge (of Scotland-yard) had the case entrusted to them, and together with the medical gentlemen engaged in the case - Dr. Bond and Dr. McCoy (assistant to Dr. Mahony, divisional police surgeon, of Commercial-road) - held consultation. A careful examination of the contents of the bundle found at Horselydown satisfied the doctors that they were portions of a body to which the leg discovered at Battersea belonged. This limb had been wrapped up in the corresponding half piece of the pair of drawers to that used for enveloping the abdominal organs, and what is regarded as a valuable clue was furnished by the linen, which was marked "L. E. Fisher." Whether this is the name of the dead woman or not the police are of course trying to ascertain, and are pursuing inquiries with the object of discovering whether a woman of that name has been missing from her friends within the last few weeks or days. In the opinion of the doctors the woman had been dead only 48 hours, and the body had then been dissected somewhat roughly by a person who nevertheless must have had some knowledge of the joints of the human body. The woman was apparently about 25 years of age, 5ft. 6in. in height, and supposed to be of fair complexion. Judging from all appearances, the police are inclined to the belief that the woman met her death by foul means. Of course in such cases suspicion is attached by some persons to the medical schools, but there is little evidence in the present case to support the idea that a practical joke has been so deliberately planned and executed. Instructions have been issued for the most careful searching of the banks of the river, so as to bring to light, if possible, the missing parts of the body. Some of the riverside watermen are of opinion that the parcels were probably thrown into the river near Vauxhall or Battersea early on Tuesday morning, and that the parcel found at Horselydown floated such a distance on account of the buoyancy of a portion of the contents. Up to midnight nothing further had transpired, notwithstanding that as long as daylight served a careful observation had been kept on the river in order to recover any of the component parts of the body which are still missing, and which may possibly yet be distributed in the bed of the Thames. It is, however, thought that these remains have not been disposed of, at least in the same vicinity as that in which the ghastly discovery was made on Tuesday; indeed if in the Thames at all. With the recent experience of the Pimlico mystery, which it will be remembered was almost identical with the present case, the authorities are disposed to encourage the belief that the remaining portions of this young woman's body will be disposed of by other means. It was not until late last evening that the examining doctors concluded their investigations. The report was then despatched to the Chief Commissioner of Police, and this was distributed late last evening throughout the metropolitan police district, in order that investigations might be established locally should there be anything to justify such a course. Meanwhile, the records of persons missing, which are preserved at headquarters, are being searched with a view of discovering whether any person answering the description of the deceased are in their possession. So far the search has been without result. The doctors' conclusion, as circulated, is to the effect that the deceased was a young woman of good physical proportions and well nourished. Her death had taken place within twenty-four hours, and there were reasons to believe that she was of superior social standing.

Search is being made at Battersea Bridge to-day for the other portions of the body, of which parts were found yesterday in the Thames. It is believed that both the parcel found at Battersea and that found at Horselydown were thrown from the Albert Bridge between six and seven o'clock yesterday morning. The thigh is found on examination to measure seventeen inches in length. The doctor is confident that the woman was alive twenty-four hours before the limb was found. It was wrapped in a piece of woman's under-garment and a piece of check ulster.

South Wales Echo - Wednesday 05 June 1889

The Ghastly Discovery in London.

LONDON, Tuesday Night. Towards the end of last year a woman's arm was found in the Thames near Westminster, and the limb was afterwards proved to belong to the decomposed trunk which was found in the cellar at the new Metropolitan Police Buildings on the Thames Embankment. That the remains were those of a murdered woman the experienced police surgeons and other officers who were engaged in the case had little, if any, doubt, but the crime remains a mystery. To-day the Thames yielded gruesome evidence of another terrible tragedy, which undoubtedly originated in crime. In two parts of the river, miles apart, were found human remains, since proved to have formed part of one body, that of a young woman, apparently about 25 years of age. The more important discovery was made at Battersea. Early this morning three lads were bathing near the Albert Bridge, on the park side, when their attention was attracted by a curious-looking object which the tide kept moving against the muddy foreshore. The lads at once went to the spot, and found, to their affright and alarm, that the object was a human limb, partly covered by a white cloth. They dressed as quickly as possible, and, wrapping the ghastly thing up as well as they could, conveyed it to the nearest police station. There it was examined by the officer in charge, and found to be a woman's thigh, perfect from the hip point to the knee, altogether about 16 inches long. The limb had been roughly and unskilfully severed from the trunk when the underclothing was still upon the body. The linen, which, being saturated by the river water, clung closely to the flesh, was examined with the hope that it might afford a clue. Upon the narrow tape waist-band was written in a clear clerkly hand in black marking ink the name, “L. E. Fisher.” Fastened in some way to the piece of linen was a square piece of black and grey check tweed. This had to all appearance belonged to a woman’s long ulster coat of good quality. It had been torn or roughly cut off, probably, the officers conjectured, from the right breast of the garment. Meanwhile the local police authorities had communicated both with Scotland Yard and the assistant divisional surgeon for Battersea. The latter gentleman, Dr Kempster, on seeing the limb, at once declared that it had not been long in the water, probably not more than twenty-four hours. That in truth was obvious even to an untrained observer, for the flesh was firm and white, and showed no signs even of the initial symptoms of putrefaction. Dr Kempster examined the limb carefully and found signs which seemed to show that previous to death the thigh had been severely bruised. Everything seemed to show that the limb was that of a fair young woman of medium height, between 20 and 25 years of age. She probably occupied a comfortable position in life.

Inspector John Tunbridge and other officers of the Criminal Investigation Department had scarcely had time to commence their investigations into the mystery of the limb when news reached Scotland Yard of another discovery of human remains, this time at St. George’s Stairs, Horselydown, a spot below London Bridge, about five miles from the scene of the first find. John Regan, a labourer, was standing on the river bank waiting for work when he noticed some boys pelting a parcel which had been left by the tide just out of the water. Regan went over to the object, and on untying the parcel found that it contained human remains. Regan handed the hideous bundle over to the Thames police, who conveyed it to Wapping police-station, where Regan told his brief story. This intelligence was sent by wire to Scotland Yard, and Dr Bond, chief surgeon to the Metropolitan police, together with several experienced detective officers, proceeded to Wapping. Dr Bond who, it may be here mentioned, has examined the remains of each of the victims of the Whitechapel fiend, saw at once that the mass of flesh before him had belonged to a young woman upon whom had been performed an unlawful operation. The remains consisted of the lower part of a female body, including the abdomen and the uterus. The flesh had been part of a living body probably 24 hours previously, for there was still a slight ooze of blood from the ragged edges where the knife or hatchet had been used. The fact that abortion had been not only attempted, but actually procured, was incontestably proved by Dr Bond. The appearance of the remains, and every point likely to be of service in the investigation which was at once commenced, were carefully written down, and the parcel was conveyed to the nearest mortuary, where it was subsequently photographed.

The limb was removed to Battersea Mortuary, and Dr Bond, who saw it, had no doubt that it belonged to the same body as did the remains found at Horselydown. If further proof of this were needed, it is to be found in the fact that part of the same under-garment as that found on the bank at Battersea was found in the parcel discovered at Horselydown. It is beyond doubt that a horrible crime has been committed. It will be learned with general satisfaction that there is reasonable ground for hope that the murderers will be brought to justice.

The unfortunate victim was probably a single woman, and she certainly met her death at the hands of a person or persons engaged in performing an unlawful operation. There are reasons, to which at present it is not advisable more particularly to refer, for believing that several persons were concerned not only in the procuration of abortion, but in the after mutilation and dismemberment. It is evident to the eyes of the experts who have seen the remains at Horselydown that the woman died from exhaustion at the very moment when the work of the criminals seemed to have been successfully accomplished. It is conjectured that the criminals, horrified and panic-stricken at the death of the victim under their very hands, hurriedly resolved to cut up the body and to dispose of it piecemeal. But with such frightened haste was the work performed that some of the most elementary precautions against detection were neglected, with the result that already the police are in possession of more than one clue which may prove of the utmost value.

Additional Details.

The Central News learns that up to a late hour to-night no further portions of the body of the murdered woman had been discovered. Barge-men, watermen, and others habitually employed on or about the river have been advised to keep a sharp look out and to report to the police as soon as they discover anything. Arrangements are also being made for a thorough and systematic search, and river experts encourage the belief that by means of experiments with the tides and currents it may be possible to arrive at an approximate idea as to the locality in which the remains were thrown into the Thames. It is considered probable that the main part of the body was buried, as in the case of the human trunk found at the new police offices last year, and search, therefore, will not be confined to the river. It is hoped that when the full reports of the crime appear in the newspapers, all persons who have friends or relatives missing will communicate with the police. Up to the present no such inquiries have been made at Scotland-yard. From a late surgical examination of the Horslyedown remains, made this evening, it has been ascertained that the murdered woman was actually delivered of a nearly full-time child, and it was her first child, as the ordinary signs of previous accouchements are all missing.

Nottingham Evening Post - Wednesday 05 June 1889

MYSTERIOUS CRIME.
MUTILATED REMAINS FOUND.

Sergeant Briggs and Sergeant Viney, who are in charge of the local inquiries at Battersea, have been busily engaged since an early hour this morning searching the foreshore of the Thames, near where the woman's thigh was found yesterday. It is believed that both that parcel, and the one found at Horsleydown, were thrown from Albert Bridge between six and seven o'clock yesterday morning, and that the parcel found at Horsleydown, by its superior buoyancy, was borne by the ebb tide down the river, while the heavier limb remained. Experiments are being conducted by the police with the object of ascertaining whether his theory is correct. A further examination of a portion of the thigh was made today in the presence of Dr. Felix Kempster and Mr. Braxton Hicks, coroner. It is the left thigh of a woman between 20 and 30 years of age. It measures 17in. in length, and the maximum and 19½ at the maximum circumference. There were four bruises as from fingers on the outer side and back of the thigh in the middle, one-third of its length. The doctor is confident that the woman was alive 24 hours before the limb was found. It was wrapped not only in the leg of a woman's under garment, but also in a piece of a woman's check ulster, torn from the bottom left hand corner, and had four button-holes in it. The whole parcel was tied with a mohair bootlace. Several inquiries have been made at Battersea Police-station to-day regarding missing friends, but as yet have thrown no light on identity of the remains.

The police attach importance to the fact that the name Fisher appears on underclothing found round the limb, and invite inquiries which may identify either the clothing or remains.

London Daily News - Thursday 06 June 1889

THE THAMES MYSTERY.
THE INQUEST.

Some further details are to hand respecting the discovery in the Thames at Battersea and Horselydown of portions of the mutilated body of a young woman. It is regarded as beyond question that a terrible crime has been committed, and there are reasons for believing that several persons were concerned not only in the unlawful operation but in the after-mutilation and dismemberment. It is believed by the experts who have seen the remains at Horselydown that the woman died from exhaustion, and that the operation, the death, and dismemberment occurred within the space of a few hours. No further portions of the body of the murdered woman have yet been discovered. It is considered probable that the main part of the body may have been buried, as in the case of a human trunk found at the new police offices last vear, and search therefore will not be confined to the river.

Mr. Wynne Baxter, the coroner for the East District of the county of London, opened an inquiry into the mystery yesterday afternoon at the Wapping Vestry Hall. - John Regan, a waterside labourer, 2, Napoleon-place, Belvedere, Bermoudsey, stated that at 10.30 on Tuesday morning he was on the shore at St. George's-stairs, Horselydown, waiting for employment. He noticed some boys throwing stones at something in the river about three yards from the shore. The boys said there were some "guts" in the parcel, and that attracted his attention to it. The witness picked it up and found that the contents were wrapped in what appeared to be a woman's apron. Finding that there pieces of flesh in the parcel the witness called the attention of some Thames policemen who were passing in a boat. They came ashore, but said that they thought the pieces of flesh were not human. The witness then picked up the pieces of flesh and replaced them in the apron. After putting them in the police boat the remains were taken to Wapping. - By the Coroner; When he first picked the pieces up they were loose in the apron. The boys emptied the apron on to the shore and then called his attention to it. He did not know the boys; there were six or seven of them. - An inspector in court said that three of the boys were known. - The inquiry was adjourned until July 3. In the meantime the remains will be removed to Battersea, where the portion of the leg found there now lies, and it is expected that the inquest will then be taken up by Mr. Braxton Hicks, the coroner for that district, who will conduct the inquiry relating to the remains now in the possession of the authorities.

South Wales Echo - Friday 07 June 1889

The Thames Mystery.
A CLUE TO THE VICTIM'S IDENTITY.

LONDON, Thursday Night. – At twenty minutes to two o'clock this afternoon a labourer named Joseph Davies discovered in Battersea Park a bundle containing some human remains, and there seems to be little doubt that these belong to the body of which the other remains recently found formed part. The bundle was discovered in a shrubbery near Park Wall. They were wrapped in a piece of brown paper, and inside was a piece of a woman's skirt of plum colour with two fringes of red and white. The band of the skirt has a blue ground with white check, and the bundle was tied with white Venetian blind cord, and some ordinary string. A large black pin was fastened to the band of the skirt, in the pocket of which was found a small black vaiganite moulded button, the surface of which is marked with parallel lines. The remains consist of the upper part of a woman's trunk, some of the ribs being missing. The breast bone has been cut nearly across. The chest cavity is empty, but the portion found contains the spleen, both kidneys and portion of the stomach and intestines. The five lower ribs are entire, and portions of the upper ones were found, but the first and second ribs are missing. The remains were removed to Battersea police station, and handed over to Sergeant Briggs, who, in conjunction with Sergeant Viney, has the local inquiries connected with the case in hand. Dr Felix Kempster, assistant divisional surgeon, was called, and he at once examined the remains. The bundle, on being opened, presented a most repulsive appearance. Shortly afterwards telegrams were despatched to the police headquarters throughout the metropolis giving the following description:- "Found today in Battersea Park, upper part of woman's trunk, probably portion of other remains found in Thames. The chest cavity was empty, but the remains consisted of the spleen, both kidneys, a portion of the stomach, a portion of the intestines, the lower six dorsal vertebrae and the upper three lumbar, five lower ribs and portions of five upper ribs, the first and second ribs being missing. There was a portion of midriff and both breasts with the [???] covering to the chest. The chest [???] is cut right down the centre, and this has apparently been done with a saw. The ribs are also sawn through in similar manner."

Dr Kempster stated to our representative that the state of decomposition in which the remains are warrants him in assuming that they belong to the body, of which portions were found in the Thames on Tuesday form part. The police hope that the further clue afforded by the mode in which the remains were packed in the parcel will materially assist them in identifying the woman, who undoubtedly has been murdered within the last few days.

Joseph Davis, in the course of an interview, said: I am a gardener employed in Battersea Park. About 20 minutes to two this afternoon I was at work there, when I saw a parcel lying among shrubs near the frame ground. This place is about 200 yards from the river shore, and is closed to the public, but people can get to a path leading to it by first climbing a low railing. The place is not much frequented by anyone employed, and the parcel might be unnoticed here for some time. When I got near the bundle I noticed a most suspicious and very unpleasant smell, and after examining it I called P.C. Angler, and together we conveyed it to the police station in a garden basket.

A Central News correspondent telegraphs:- Another bundle of human remains was discovered just before two o'çlock on Thursday afternoon in a somewhat secluded shrubbery in Battersea Park, which is close to the spot where the thigh of a woman was found on Tuesday. That limb, it will be remembered, was wrapped in a portion of an undergarment, upon which was written the name "L. E. Fisher," and there is no reason to doubt that the remains now discovered belonged to the same body as the limb and the abdomen and other organs found at Horselydown. Previous to the discovery in Battersea Park the river police had been dragging the water near Vauxhall Bridge. About noon they fished up the neck, shoulder, the first and second ribs, and the liver. These have been examined and pronounced to be part of the same body as the other portions. All that remains to be found now in order to piece the various parts into a complete whole are the head, the two arms, one thigh, and two legs from the knee downwards. Of these, the most important of course is the head. The presumption is that this has been burned; but the general recklessness shown by the murderers affords some ground for hope that they may have neglected even such an obvious precaution as the destruction of the head, or the complete mutilation of the features of their victim.

A later telegram says:- The investigations so far made into the Thames mystery have resulted not only in finding many portions of the body, but have furnished the police with particulars which inspire the hope of their being able to establish the identity of the deceased woman. The Metropolitan police have, amongst numerous enquiries made after lost friends, received a letter from Oxford to the effect that the murdered woman is supposed to be L. E. Fisher, a native of that city. The letter states that the published description of the remains is almost identical with the personal appearance of this young woman, who came to London for the purpose of entering service in a good family some time ago.

Lloyd's Weekly Newspaper - Sunday 09 June 1889

THE THAMES MYSTERY.
MORE REMAINS FOUND YESTERDAY.

Shortly before eight o'clock yesterday morning, a man employed as a wharf labourer, near London- bridge, picked up a parcel which he found floating in the river Thames off the Bankside. He called Sub-inspector Knight, of the Thames police, who took charge of the bundle, and took it to the police- station, where it was handed over to Inspector Dennis, who at once called in Dr. Kempster, divisional surgeon for the district. He examined the parcel, and found it contained the left arm, forearm and hand of a female with fair skin. There was light auburn hair on the arm-pit; the limb was shapely and there were no marks of rings on the fingers, so it is believed from this fact that the woman was unmarried. The arm was disjointed at the shoulder joint by a clean cut. There were vaccination scars on the upper part. Dr. Kempster is of opinion, judging from the state of decomposition and the colour of the hair, that it is part of the same body of which remains have already been discovered. The hand is well-shaped and evidently that of a person in a superior position of life, as the nails appear to have been well cared for and the whole limb is very clean. The limb was wrapped in a small piece of brown paper, was bent at the elbow joint, and the bend tied by a piece of common string.

Palmer, interviewed, said:- "When I noticed that something was floating in the river, I said to Chudleigh that I thought it looked very much like a portion of the body which the police are looking for. He replied he did not think so, and that it was a dead cat. I got a broom and turned it over, and saw it had fingers. I told Chudleigh it was an arm, and he picked it out of the water. There was a piece of string which tied the arm together in a bent position. It had been cut off at the shoulder with a sharp knife, and there was no sign of hacking. It was the left arm, and seemed to me to be that of a woman. We hailed a police boat, and the police at once rowed over and took possession of the limb."

About a quarter to one yesterday afternoon another portion of the body was picked up in the Thames off

Battersea steamboat pier. It consisted of the buttocks and bony pelvis. The remains, which were uncovered, were conveyed to the Battersea mortuary, and Dr. Kempster, the police divisional surgeon, was called to examine them. He found that the skin, which had been somewhat irregularly cut, fitted in with the other parts. All the organs of the bony pelvis were missing, the bladder being cut through in the pubic arch. A careful examination supported the early theory of the medical gentlemen, that the deceased woman had recently given birth to a child. A curious point is that a piece of fine linen - about 9½in. by 8in. - probably a handkerchief, was found rolled and pushed into the body. The whole skin and the front of the pelvis were absent, and this was found to be supplied by the portion of the body found at Horselydown on Tuesday last.

Another discovery was made during the day by a newspaper reporter, he finding in the garden of Sir Percy Shelley's house at Chelsea (just by the river) the missing right thigh. The limb, which was very much decomposed, was disjointed at the hip and knee in the same manner as the other thigh. It was close upon 17 inches in length. The knee-cap was not missing, and judging from certain indications, the doctors' opinion that the deceased woman had auburn hair was corroborated. The cut apparently had been made by a person possessing some knowledge of anatomy. The limb was wrapped in a piece of ulster, in which other remains had been found, as well as what appears to be the pocket of an apron, similar to those used by meat or fish salesmen.

Shelley house was formerly in the occupation of Sir Percy Shelley, but he removed some time ago, and it is now rented by Sir Arthur Charles, who is at present in the Isle of Wight.

The Central News says:- We have received the following authoritative description of the chief portions found yesterday. The portion found floating in the river consisted of the buttocks and pelvis, and two lower lumber vertebrae, which were missing from the parts previously found. The trunk is now perfect. The skin on the buttocks is perfect, and fits with the skin and the back portion found in Battersea on the 6th inst. All the pelvis viscera are missing. The pieces found at Horselydown fit exactly, and the hair corresponds. The two thighs both fit, and the cut edges of the skin match. There are no bruises about the skin. The right thigh is disjointed, the hip and knee joint about 17 inches in length. The thigh fits the pelvis, as does also the right leg, which was found on Friday. The knee-cap of this leg is uninjured." The Central News adds:- "In strange contrast to the coarse costermonger's pocket found with the thigh discovered at Shelley house, a small square of fine linen was fastened to the buttocks."

Great hopes are entertained that the missing head will soon come to light, as the decomposition of the brain, which proceeds very quickly, will give the skull sufficient buoyancy to float, provided, of course, it has not been placed in a heavily weighted parcel.

The inquest will be held at the Star and Garter inn, Church-street, Battersea, but the date is uncertain. Coroner Braxton Hicks will hold the inquiry.

The police are constantly in receipt of communications from persons who have lost sight of friends and relatives. A report set in circulation of an Oxford woman being the victim is contradicted.

The police also received an intimation that the victim might be a Laura E. Fisher, formerly a barmaid at the Old Cock tavern and refreshment rooms, Highbury. This young woman, however, has been discovered living at Ramsgate.

A constable in the Herts constabulary named Fisher stated that he believed the remains were those of his sister, whose maiden name was L. B. Fisher. It appears that just previous to her marriage she marked a quantity of her linen with that name. She married a man named Wren, and went to live at Hornsey, but a little over a year ago she eloped with a man named Robinson, a plasterer by trade. Nothing had since been heard of her or of Robinson.

A circumstance has occurred at Leman-street police-station which was at first regarded as a hoax, but which, from subsequent events. has received more attention. Two or three days previous to the discovery of human remains in the Thames, a letter was received stating that it was the writer's intention to "recommence operations in that neighbourhood shortly." The police now believe that, anticipating the discovery of human remains. This letter was written in a clumsy attempt to make the murder appear to have been committed by the author of the Whitechapel outrages. Other letters have since been received at the same police-station, evidently in the same handwriting, and all bearing the London post-mark, and the police are making an endeavour to trace the writer.

The police announce that the portions of clothing which have been found have been carefully preserved at Battersea police-station, Bridge-road, where they will be open between the hours of 10 and four, for the inspection of any individuals who have missing female friends. The left thigh was wrapped in a piece of black and grey check tweed ulster. The lower part of the abdomen was wrapped in the left leg of the same pair of drawers on which the name was written. The trunk was wrapped in a square piece of brown paper, and a portion of a dark plush coloured skirt with two flounces. The police, in reference to this, wish it to be noticed that this skirt had a band made of a material with blue ground and a white check, tied with Venetian blue cord and a piece of ordinary string. The portion which was picked up yesterday morning off Battersea steam-boat pier was wrapped in a cambric handkerchief. The right thigh found in a garden near the Chelsea embankment was wrapped in what had been a woman's pocket made of blue and white check.

Lloyd's Weekly Newspaper - Sunday 09 June 1889

LONDON'S LATEST HORROR.

For a parallel to the horrible mystery of the Thames which is now exciting the public mind, it is necessary to go back to the beginning of the year 1837. It was then that Greenacre scattered about London parts of the dismembered body of Hannah Browne; and their gradual discovery led to the monster being hunted down and executed. Anything more ghastly than the record of the picking up day after day of the human fragments cannot well be imagined; but the widest publicity will, we trust, prove the surest aid to the detection of the atrocious crime. The following are the portions found;-

TUESDAY.-	Left leg and thigh, off Battersea. Lower part of abdomen, at Horselydown.
THURSDAY.-	The liver, near Nine-elms. Upper part of body, in Battersea-park. Neck and shoulders, off Battersea.
FRIDAY.-	Right foot and part of leg, Wandsworth. Left leg and foot, at Limehouse.
SATURDAY.-	Left arm and hand, at Bankside. Buttocks and bony pelvis, off Battersea. Right thigh, Chelsea-embankment.

The portions now missing are the head and neck, right arm and hand, lungs and heart, and intestines.

Yesterday afternoon we received the following, dated "4, Whitehall-place, June 8":-

"The Commissioner of Police of the Metropolis presents his compliments to the Editor, and begs to ask that the enclosed facsimile of the name on the portion of a pair of women's drawers in which part of the human remains recently found in the river Thames was wrapped, may be reproduced in Lloyd's."

The specimen sent showed the name in white letters on a black ground; but as it was really written in black marking ink on the white under-garment, we had it cut in metal, and are thus able to meet Commissioner Monro's wishes by giving the following facsimile:-

L. E. Fisher

Any information likely to lead to the identity of the victim should be at once sent to the police at Scotland-yard.

Illustrated Police News - Saturday 15 June 1889

GHASTLY DISCOVERIE'S IN THE THAMES.

PORTIONS OF THE BODY AT HORSLEYDOWN

DISCOVERY OF HUMAN REMAINS IN BATTERSEA-PARK.

ALBERT BRIDGE.

South Wales Daily News - Monday 17 June 1889

THE THAMES MYSTERY.
OPENING OF THE INQUEST.
THE MEDICAL EVIDENCE.

On Saturday an inquest was opened at the Star and Garter, Battersea, opposite the Church of St. Mary-by-the-River, by Mr Braxton Hicks, on the mutilated remains of a young woman found in Battersea Park, on the Chelsea Embankment, and in the Thames during several preceding days. These remains, by medical report, are those of a young woman, aged from 24 to 26 years; height, 5ft. 4in.; well built and fleshy; very fair skin; hair, light brown or sandy; and well-shaped hands and feet. All the principal portions of the body have been discovered excepting the head, and upon certain fragments of clothes in which the limbs were wrapped "L. E. Fisher" was found marked. Inspector Tunbridge appeared on behalf of the police authorities.

The coroner informed the jury that the first portion of the remains was found on Tuesday week, at a quarter to nine, in the Battersea Park, and the second portion at Horselydown at half-past ten. All the portions subsequently discovered had been brought into his district and placed together in the mortuary, where the jury had seen them. The case was a most serious one, and would require their careful consideration.

The first witness called was Mr Thomas Bond, F.R.C.S., surgeon to Westminster Hospital. He said he was requested by the Assistant-Commissioner of Police to examine the remains. He had since done so, and had prepared a report. Dr Bond then proceeded to read the report, which was very lengthy. He was of opinion that the woman had not been dead more than 24 hours when he examined the first remains found. The woman had not been delivered at the time of death, and the child was, he believed, removed after death, and there was no evidence to show whether the woman died a violent or a natural death. The various joints were neatly divided, all the organs were healthy, and there were no marks of violence previous to death. There was nothing to indicate the cause of death. Deceased had not performed hard work, as there was no thickening of the skin in the palm of the hand; the nails were close pared or bitten down; there were four vaccination marks on the left arm. Measurements of the several portions found were then given. There were no marks, scars, or bruises upon the body, except a mark on the ring finger on the left hand, which must have been caused by the removal of the ring after death. The conclusions he had formed were that deceased was alive 24 hours before the first remains were found; that deceased was fair, plump, well formed, and well nourished, and was at the time of death seven or eight months advanced in pregnancy. She was from 23 to 25 years of age, and 5ft. 4in. to 5ft. 6in. in height. The parts had been severed with skill and design, but not with the anatomical skill of a surgeon. What skill was shown was the technical skill of a butcher or horse knacker, or of a person accustomed to deal with dead animals. There was a great similarity of design in the case with what is known as the Rainham mystery and the remains found under the new police offices on the Embankment. In those cases no head was found.

Dr Felix Kempster, of Bridge-road, Battersea, gave evidence which corresponded with that previously given by Mr Bond. He examined a thigh on the 4th inst. at the Battersea Police-Station, other portions on the 6th and 7th, and he entirely agreed with the observations made and the conclusions arrived at by Dr Bond. On subsequent days he made examinations of other portions, and found that they fitted exactly. In a pocket about one portion be found a black vulcanite button, and a similar button was found upon a portion of dress wrapped about another fragment of the same body. When he first examined the ring finger there was no bruise, but one appeared later on, and was noticed by him upon subsequent examination.

This concluded the medical evidence, and the next witnesses were those who had discovered the several remains, in order to trace their removal to the mortuary at Battersea.

Some other evidence having been given, the inquiry was adjourned until July 1.

SEARCHING FOR REMAINS.
A DOG UTILISED BY THE POLICE.

The Central News says:- An attempt was made on Sunday morning by means of a dog to discover the head of the woman whose mutilated remains have been found recently in the Thames and elsewhere. The police are extremely anxious to obtain this most important link to the woman's identification in order to increase their chances of bringing the miscreants to justice. It will be remembered that on the occasion when the remains of a mutilated woman were found in some vaults near the

Embankment that a dog belonging to Mr Waring, named Smoker, was utilised and was instrumental in finding some of the missing parts after the police search bad been practically abandoned. The same dog was utilised on this occasion. Mr Waring, the owner; Sergeant Briggs, who shouldered a rusty shovel and a reporter of the Central News set out from Battersea Police-station at half-past five. The animal was taken to the thicket in Battersea Park where some of the remains had been found previously, and was put on the spot where the parcel had lain. The dog immediately became interested, and worked the whole plantation thoroughly, smelling the earth, and finally running beside the nursery wall which skirts this particular thicket. At one spot where the dog seemed more than usually interested, Sergeant Briggs turned up the sewer, and some suspicious-looking substance, in a state of decomposition, was brought to light, but a closer examination proved this to be undoubtedly of vegetable origin. After an hour and a half's work the search was reluctantly abandoned, it being generally agreed that the time which had been allowed to lapse since the discovery in the Park before this experiment was made had greatly militated against its success. It is the opinion of the police that the head of the victim has either been burned or buried, and the scene of the crime is believed to have been either Chelsea or Battersea. From the fact that no woman has been reported missing who at all answers to the description of the victim, it is considered probable that she was a recent arrival in London, without friends. Another theory is that the woman's friends may have made themselves accessories to the crime in the first instance, by arranging for an illegal operation to be performed upon her, and are now keeping quiet for their safety sake. If, as is now believed probable, the women found mutilated at Rainham and on the Embankment met their deaths in the same way as this latest victim, it is evident that there exists in London an establishment where illegal operations upon women are regularly performed, and to the discovery of this the police are directing all their attention.

London Evening Standard - Monday 17 June 1889

THE DISCOVERY OF REMAINS.

An inquest was opened on Saturday at the Star and Garter, Battersea, by Mr. Braxton Hicks, Coroner for Mid-Surrey, on the mutilated remains of a young woman found in Battersea Park, on the Chelsea Embankment, and in the Thames, during several preceding days.

Inspector Tunbridge appeared on behalf of the police authorities.

The Coroner informed the Jury that the first portion of the remains was found on Tuesday week, at a quarter to nine, in Battersea Park, and the second portion at Horselydown, at half-past ten. All the portions subsequently discovered had been brought into his district and placed together in the mortuary where the Jury had seen them.

Mr. Thomas Bond, surgeon to the A Division of police, stated that he was called on June 4 by Mr. Anderson, Assistant Commissioner of Police, to examine some remains of a human body at Battersea and Wapping. He first went to Battersea, where he examined a human thigh. Since then he had examined other portions lying in the mortuary. The thigh was the left one, and had been severed with three or more sweeping excisions from the hip joint. The head of the thigh bone had been neatly disarticulated, and so had the lower portion. He considered that the remains had only been severed a few hours. There were traces of blood. On the same day he examined four portions of the abdomen at Wapping Police-court, and gave a minute description of what he noticed. The remains were those of a woman very recently delivered, but after death. In his opinion, the woman had not been dead twenty-four hours when he examined the remains. The child was the first borne by the Deceased. He could not tell whether death was the result of violence or from natural causes; but the body had been cut up soon after death. On the 7th of June, in conjunction with Mr. Hibbard and Mr. Kempster, he made a further examination of other portions of a human body - the shoulders, upper part of the back, and also the lower part of the back. The portions showed that the severances were made by a skilled hand; and the parts fitted with those portions previously found and lying in the mortuary. Upon June 8 he made, in conjunction with the same medical men, further examinations of two legs and feet found, and came to the conclusion that they were portions of the same body. Again, on the 10th inst, he made examinations of further portions, all of which had been cleverly disarticulated. They belonged to the same body, and proved that the Deceased was not delivered before death. The hands showed that the Deceased had not performed hard work, as there was no thickening of the skin in the palm of the hand; the nails were close pared or bitten down; there were four vaccination marks on the left arm. Measurements of the several portions found were then given. There were no marks, scars, or bruises upon the body, except a mark on the ring finger of the left hand, which must have been caused by the removal of the ring after death. The conclusions he had formed were that deceased was alive 24 hours before the first remains were found, that deceased was fair, plump, well formed, and well nourished, and was at the time of death seven or eight mouths advanced in pregnancy. She was from 23 to 25 years of age, and 5ft. 4in. to 5ft 6in. in height. The parts had been severed with skill and design, but not with the anatomical skill of a surgeon. What skill was shown was the technical skill of a butcher or horse knacker, or of a person accustomed to deal with dead animals. There was a great similarity of design in the case with what was known as the Rainham mystery, and the remains found under the new Police-offices on the Embankment. In these cases no head was found.

Dr. Felix Kempster, of Bridge-road, Battersea, next gave evidence, which corresponded with that previously given by Dr. Bond. He examined a thigh on the 4th inst. at the Battersea Police-station, other portions on the 6th and 7th, and he entirely agreed with the observations made and the conclusions arrived at by Dr. Bond. On subsequent days he made examinations of other portions, and found that they fitted exactly. In a pocket about one portion he found a black vulcanite button, and a similar button was found upon a portion of dress wrapped about another fragment of the same body. When he first examined the ring finger there was no bruise, but one appeared later on, and was noticed by him upon subsequent examination.

This concluded the medical evidence, and the Coroner stated that the next witnesses would be those who had discovered the several remains, in order to trace their removal to the mortuary at Battersea.

Isaac Brett, 15, a little porter at a wood shop, living at 7, Laurence-street, said he was bathing under the Albert Bridge, on the 4th, between eight and nine, when he saw a parcel against a barge. He took it up, and put it on the steps leading to the road. A gentleman looked at it, and told Witness to take it to the police-station, and he did so. The parcel was on the shore, near to the Park.

Serjeant Briggs, V Division, deposed that on the 4th the last Witness gave him a bundle, which contained the left thigh of a woman. It was wrapped in a portion of a woman's ulster and drawers.

Patrick McCarthy, eleven years of age, living at 13, Howell's-place, Horselydown, deposed that on Tuesday week, between ten and eleven in the morning, he found a parcel in the river, near George's Stairs. The parcel was just moving about; it contained “some flesh:” and another boy told the police, and a Thames policeman took it off. It was wrapped in an apron. The tide was going down at the time.

Alfred Freshwater, of the Thames Police, stationed at Wapping, was in the police boat on the morning named, and was called to the shore at Horselydown, where a parcel containing human remains was handed to him. He placed it in the boat and conveyed it to Wapping

Station. The portion found could be brought down on the one tide; it was given to him about 10.30 a.m.

Joseph Davies, gardener, employed at Battersea Park, of 15, Randle-street, on the 6th inst. found a parcel in the park, at the back of the frame garden, in the shrubbery, at about two in the afternoon. Only the gardeners had admission to that part of the park, but anybody else could get over the fencing. The bundle was 25 yards away from the fence. He called Police-constable Anger, who took the parcel away. The wicket-gate of the park was opened at five a.m., and that would be 200 yards away from where the parcel was found. All the gates of the park were opened at the same time in the morning. The wicket-gate was close to the Albert Bridge, and there was no one on duty at that point.

Police-constable Anger, 500 V, said he was called to the park about 2.00 p.m. on the 6th inst., and was shown a parcel which contained a portion of the trunk of a woman. He took it to the police-station, and from there to the mortuary.

Claude Mellor, a newspaper reporter, St. Oswald's-road, Fulham, said on the 8th inst. he was on the Chelsea Embankment, having landed from a steamer, about noon, and saw a parcel lying in the garden of Sir Percy Shelley's house. An inspector of police came up, and the parcel was removed. The parcel must have been thrown over the railings, because, in falling, some branches of a bush beneath which the parcel lay had been broken off.

Charles Marlow, barge builder, 15, Wye-street Battersea, stated that at four o'clock on the afternoon of the 6th he saw a parcel floating in the river, opposite Covington's Wharf. It was about 100 yards from the shore; he secured it and brought it ashore. The parcel contained the upper portion of a human body.

Edward Stanton, waterman, of 73, Park-street, Limehouse, said that he found, on the 7th inst. about half-past nine in the morning, the left thigh and foot of a human being floating in the Thames, near the West India Dock Buoy. He handed it over to the Thames Police.

Solomon Hearne, tinman and brazier, whose address was, "living in a tent near a dust-heap on Lammas-land, Townmead-road, Fulham," stated that on the 7th, about four o'clock in the morning, he found a leg and foot on the shore near Wandsworth Bridge, upon the Middlesex side of the shore.

W. J. Chidley, a lighterman, of 4, Adelaide-place, Borough-market, saw an arm and hand about a quarter to eight on the morning of the 8th, floating off the Phoenix Wharf, Bankside. He recovered the remains and handed them to the police.

Inspector Churcher, Thames Police, stationed at Waterloo, said on the 8th, about 12.25 p.m., in the mid-channel between the Albert Suspension Bridge and Battersea Park Pier, he saw floating some human remains, which he conveyed to Battersea. They were declared by Dr. Kempster to be a portion of the body of a female.

Joseph Squires, lighterman, living in Westminster, on the 10th inst., about half-past twelve, found the right arm of a body floating in the river near Newton's Wharf, Bankside. He gave it to Police-constable Trent, who deposed that he took the remains to the mortuary at Battersea. There was some string tied round the arm.

David King, an engineer, living in Nine-elms, on the 6th inst., about half-past seven in the morning, found some remains floating in the river off Palace Wharf, Nine-elms, which he handed over to Police-constable Bransgrove, of the Thames Police, stationed at Waterloo, and they were afterwards brought to Battersea by Inspector Law, who gave evidence to that effect.

Joseph Goodman, labourer, on the 7th instant, found human remains floating in the river, off Palace Wharf, about nine in the morning, and these were taken to the mortuary by Police-constable Hall, 407 W.

Serjeant Briggs identified the fragments of clothing produced as being the fragments found in the several remains brought to the mortuary. The button in the dress pocket did not correspond with the buttons found on the ulster. All the other materials corresponded, as though they had been worn by the same individual.

Inspector Tunbridge said they were still pursuing their inquiries; and he had no further evidence ready that day.

The inquiry was adjourned until July 1.

Hull Daily Mail - Wednesday 26 June 1889

THE THAMES MYSTERY. IDENTIFICATION OF THE BODY. A SUPPOSED VICTIM OF "JACK THE RIPPER."

After more than a fortnight of patient and unremitting inquiries and investigation, the Metropolitan Police have at length been able to place practically beyond doubt the identity of the woman, the portions of whose mutilated remains have been found in the Thames from time to time since the 4th inst. All important portions of the body, with the exception of the head, are still preserved in spirit at the Battersea Mortuary. It was feared that in the absence of the head it would be impossible to establish the identity of the unfortunate victim of what was evidently a foul crime; but by means of certain scars, and by the portions of clothing incautiously or recklessly left by murderer, a number of persons have been enabled to declare in the most positive manner that the murdered woman was Elizabeth Jackson, a homeless woman, well known in some of the common lodging-houses in the Chelsea district.

Elizabeth Jackson was last seen alive on the 31st of May. Since then she has not been in any of her accustomed haunts, and a number of convergent facts in the possession of the police leave little doubt that upon the evening of that day the wretched woman met her murderer. The various articles of clothing found with portions of the body have been identified by a number of women who knew Elizabeth Jackson intimately, and were in fact her companions. All identified them without hesitation as having belonged to Jackson, who it appears was also pretty well known to the police in the Chelsea district. The police on their part traced the woman's movements to the hour almost of her disappearance. She certainly has not since been any of the many common lodging-houses, nor an inmate of any of the casual wards, workhouses, or hospitals in London. Living from hand to mouth she must have been without means to leave London except on foot, and her physical condition made it practically impossible for her to go on tramp. She disappeared on the evening of the 31st of May, and upon the morning of the 4th of June the first of the dreadful discoveries was made at Battersea and at Horselydown.

It is noteworthy that the houses in which Elizabeth Jackson lodged from time to time and the thoroughfares which she used mostly to frequent are all within a short distance of Battersea Bridge, whence the lighter parts of the body were evidently thrown into the river, and Battersea Park, where the upper portion of the trunk was found. There is even reason to believe that the murder was committed in a lonely part of the park after the gates had been close for the night. The murderer, locked in with the girl, would have little difficulty completing the ghastly work of dismemberment before daylight, supposing he had previously provided himself with the necessary implements. There is, in truth serious ground for connecting the murder of Elizabeth Jackson with the Whitechapel atrocities, which startled London on and off all last year. Indeed, there were certain mutilations of the corpse which, though it was thought desirable at the time to suppress them, immediately suggested the handiwork of that most monstrous of murderers. The theory that the victim died from the effects of an unlawful operation performed upon her has been altogether abandoned.

Shields Daily Gazette - Wednesday 26 June 1889

THE THAMES MYSTERY.
THE REMAINS IDENTIFIED.
STATEMENT BY DECEASED'S SISTER.

The Central News understands that the clue first taken up by the police was that afforded by the name "E. L. Fisher," which was written in marking ink on tbe band of the undergarment found on the first portion of the body found at Battersea. It was ascertained that the garment originally belonged to a lady in a good position in society, who, upon her marriage some five or six years ago, gave it away with other cast-off underclothing and wearing apparel. The police traced the garment from owner to owner until they found the person who gave it to the missing woman, Elizabeth Jackson. Among the other evidences of identification was that furnished by the sister of Jackson, who stated that her missing sister had a peculiar scar on one of her wrists. The remains in Battersea Mortuary were in consequence of this statement again examined by Dr Bond, Dr Hibbert, and Dr Felix Kempster. The flesh of the wrist was somewhat decomposed, but on lifting the skin the experts mentioned arrived at the conclusion that a scar similar to that described by the sister had certainly existed.

OTHER TESTIMONY.

A woman known as Sally, who lived at Sharpe's boarding house in Turk's Row, says that Elizabeth Jackson told her when she last saw her about five or six weeks ago, that she thought she was about to become a mother. This agrees with the opinion formed by the surgeons who conducted the post-mortem examination. Jackson's favourite promenade was in Battersea Park, off which portions of her remains were found. She often walked there at nights. Several weeks ago the police approached Sally, and made inquiries about the whereabouts of Jackson. She was, however, unable to give them any information. The description furnished by the police of the woman whose remains were found in the Thames coincided exactly with that of Jackson. The latter was twenty-three years old, fair, and about five feet six or seven inches in height. She was certainly thin in the face, but not by any means so as to other parts of the body, being plump rather than otherwise. Sally knew the man with whom Jackson was living, and another man, probably a detective, was looking for him less than three weeks ago. Ada, another inhabitant of Turk's Row, knew Jackson's walk, and last saw her about five weeks ago. She was then dressed in some dark-coloured dress, and wore an ulster, black and gray in colour, a kind of check pattern. Jackson used to wear a brass ring on one of her fingers. She bad given way to drink since Christmas. The woman Sally says the police told her they were Jackson's remains which had been found. It is noteworthy that the houses in which Elizabeth Jackson lodged from time to time, and the thoroughfares which she used to promenade at night, are all within a short distance of Battersea Bridge, whence the lighter parts of the body were evidently thrown into the river, and Battersea Park, where the upper portion of the trunk was found.

There is every reason to believe that the murder was even committed in a lonely part of the park after tbe gates had closed for the night. Jackson used to boast to her acquaintances that she sometimes remained in the park at night long after it had been closed to the public. After the successful accomplishment of the murder the murderer would have little difficulty in completing the ghastly work of dismemberment before daylight, supposing he had previously provided himself with the necessary implements. There is in truth serious ground for connecting the murder of Elizabeth Jackson with the Whitechapel atrocities which startled London on and off all last year. A woman named Forster has identified a button which she herself sewed on the ulster of the deceased woman. It was in the ulster that portion of the remains was wrapped. The utmost difficulty is experienced obtaining information from the deceased's relations and other persons knowing something of her antecedents, who have been requested by the police to be very reticent on the subject whilst investigations are in progress.

ANOTHER VICTIM OF JACK THE RIPPER.

The Central News says various circumstances connected with the fate of Elizabeth Jackson lead to the belief that she was really a victim of the Whitechapel fiend, Jack the Ripper. Weeks ago we were in possession of information respecting a nameless indignity inflicted upon the victim's corpse, which it was then considered advisable to suppress in the published reports. That indignity was of a character instinctively to suggest the handiwork of the most monstrous of murders. It may be assumed that the police authorities have abandoned the theory that the victim died from the effects of an unlawful operation performed upon her. Elizabeth Jackson had no necessity to resort to abortion, for she had no shame to hide, and no professional performer of illegal operations would risk his neck for the sake of a penniless woman. It has been discovered that a millstone dresser, who cohabited with the deceased, has left the neighbourhood and is being sought for by the police.

The Star - Saturday 29 June 1889

THE THAMES MYSTERY.

The Press Association says:- The possibility of the mystery surrounding the discovery of human remains in the Thames at the beginning of the present month is by no means remote; in fact, the police are gaining ground each day in their endeavours to trace the identity of the victim and the origin of the crime. The supposed victim, Elizabeth Jackson, is a native of Chelsea, and is very well known in and about the neighbourhood of Pimlico. Elizabeth Jackson was born in the neighbourhood of Cheyne-place, but, as far as can be ascertained at present, it is only during the past four or five years that she has lived a precarious and degraded life. It was on the 21st of the present month that the police obtained their first clue to the supposed victim, and also to a man named John Fairclough who cohabited with her. The last house at which Jackson was known was a common lodging-house, 10, Turks-row, Pimlico-road, near the Chelsea Barracks. She remained at this house only two or three days, when she left for other unknown quarters, says Mr. Willing, the deputy, on Wednesday, May 21st, in consequence of her mother having taken lodgings in the same house. Nothing more was seen of her until two days later, when "Ginger Nell," one of the lodgers at Mr. Willing's, saw her standing at the corner of Turk's-row. She was in a very dirty condition and complained that she had no money to get lodgings. On being asked by "Ginger Nell" where she had been she replied "Sleeping on the seats on the Chelsea Embankment." She further stated that she walked about at night in the neighbourhood of the Albert Palace and Albert Bridge. She was warned against a dangerous class of boatmen, who infested the district, but she did not appear to heed the advice. This appears to be the last that ever was seen of her, until her remains were found at various points in the Thames. Several persons have identified the piece of ulster in which one of the limbs was wrapped as belonging to the ulster worn by the Deceased when she disappeared. Regarding the piece of drawers bearing the name "L. E. Fisher," in which the limb found at Horselydown was wrapped it has been ascertained (it is stated to-day) that they were purchased by the Deceased after she left Turks-row, as on that occasion "Ginger Nell" states she was not possessed of such a garment. There is now every reason to suppose that the surmise that the Deceased fell a victim to an abortionist is incorrect. There is corroborative testimony that the Deceased was murdered by a person or persons with a seafaring knowledge. Who were these individuals? The Deceased had been warned of a certain class of men who took advantage of and liberties with unfortunates in the vicinity of Battersea Bridge. These men comprise two classes, Thames bargemen and engine cleaners. Both are said to be dangerous classes to this district. It will be remembered that when the bony pelvis, one of the last of the Battersea discoveries, was found, it was plugged in such a manner as to leave absolutely no doubt that the murder had been committed by, or assisted in by, a man with an extensive marine knowledge; therefore, in view of these facts, the police are directing their attention to the Thames, in the hope of discovering the secret of the mystery, which they feel confident is concealed there. Regarding the man John Fairclough, active search is being made for him - not that it is supposed that he is concerned in the crime, but in order that he may assist the police in discovering Elizabeth Jackson's antecedents, such of those as are not already known to Jackson's friends who have been found. The continued absence of the man is creating some suspicion in official circles, but it is not thought improbable that he will be speedily tracked, as he has already been traced, it is stated, to the Isle of Dogs. The suggestion that the girl was murdered within the precincts of Battersea Park is ridiculed by the authorities, it being thought more probable that the scene of the murder was aboard a Thames boat.

SUPPOSED IMPORTANT CLUE.

What is supposed to be an important clue to this mystery is reported by the East Anglian Daily Times as establishing the identity of the woman Jackson with a person who lived with a man named Fairclough at Ipswich some time ago. “In the early part of January last, Fairclough, with a woman, who passed as his wife, took rooms in Princes-street, in that town. Fairclough obtained work as a stone-dresser at St. Peter's Foundry, where he was looked upon as a decent-sort of fellow. At home, however, he bore a very different character. Both Fairclough and the woman are described as being exceedingly close with regard to their previous life, but in the course of casual conversations, Fairclough let the fact ooze out that originally he came from Lancashire, joined the 2nd Battalion Grenadier Guards at Windsor (from which he deserted), was captured and sentenced to a term of imprisonment, and afterwards discharged from the army on account of deafness. The woman, too, rarely spoke of her antecedents, beyond mentioning that she at one time was in service, which she left for the purpose of joining Fairclough when he came to Ipswich. Here their life was a most unhappy one. Their quarrelling was incessant and in their mutual recrimination the woman persistently maintained that Fairclough was a deserter, and she would call in the police and have him arrested. This, however, she never attempted to do although at times she was most unnaturally used, and on one occasion was badly wounded in the arm by a knife thrust from Fairclough. Latterly she admitted to a Mrs. Connolly, who lived in the same house, that her name was Jackson, and that Fairclough was not her husband. A letter, in fact, came to the house addressed to Jackson, and which she claimed. In the course of the quarrels, Jackson taunted Fairclough that if she was in London he dared not assault her. He is also said to have been jealous of the woman, who, however, is believed while in Ipswich to have lead a respectable life; indeed, she rarely went out, although at times she suffered the pinches of poverty. In this way the couple lived up to the 31st March last, when, without giving any warning either to the landlady or the inmates, they left the premises, and have not been seen since in Ipswich. It was then ascertained that sheets and other portable property belonging to the landlady had been disposed of.

Exeter and Plymouth Gazette - Tuesday 02 July 1889

THE THAMES MYSTERY.

Mr. A. Braxton Hicks, the Mid-Surrey coroner, resumed his inquiry yesterday, at the Star and Garter, Battersea, into the circumstances attending the death of a woman whose mutilated remains were discovered in various parts of the Thames, in Battersea Park, and on the Chelsea Embankment in the early part of last month. - Inspector Tunbridge and Detective-sergeant Briggs again appeared to watch the case on behalf of the Criminal Investigation Department - The first witness called was Frederick Chinn, a policeman of the T Division, stationed at Fulham. He stated that on June 7th he received a foot and leg from Inspector Brown and handed it to the coroner's officer. - Caroline Jackson, a married woman, living in the Chelsea Workhouse, said that she had a daughter named Elizabeth, who was 24 years of age last March. Witness last saw her on May 31st. She was about 5ft. 5in. in height, well formed and plump, and when witness saw her last she had not been doing much work. Witness had never even her bite her nails. She had a beautiful set of teeth, was very fair, and she had golden hair. On May 31st she saw her in Queen's-road, Chelsea, and her daughter ran away the moment she caught sight of her. She caught up to her, however, and asked her why she had run away, and she replied that she was ashamed to see her. They were together all that afternoon. Witness had not seen her since October. They separated at 8.30, but the girl did not say where she was going. She was wearing an ulster exactly similar to the piec of material produced. Witness was able to identify ths button on the sleeve of the ulster, also produced by Detective Briggs. Her daughter told witness that she was expecting to be confined in the first week in September. She said she was living with a man named Jack Faircloth, a stonemason, who, she added, was the father of her child. She explained that she came from Ipswich with Faircloth, and that after living for some time at Poplar they went to Battersea, where he left her, after promising to come home to dinner. In reply to the coroner, witness said that her daughter had been in service. It was always in the neighbourhoods of Chelsea and Fulham that she was in service. She was a virtuous girl down to about seven months since. The only man whose name she mentioned was Faircloth. She had a scar underneath one of her arms, the result of a cut from a vase about 12 years ago, when she was living at home.

Western Daily Press - Tuesday 02 July 1889

THE THAMES MYSTERY.
THE INQUEST.

The inquest on the remains of the woman found in the Thames, and who has since been identified as Elizabeth

Jackson, was resumed before Mr Braxton Hicks, the coroner at Battersea, yesterday.

After further evidence as to the picking up of the remains,

Mrs Caroline Jackson, a very respectable-looking woman, said that, together with her husband, she was an inmate of the Chelsea Workhouse. She had a daughter named Elizabeth Jackson, who was twenty-four on the 18th March last. She last saw her alive on the 31st of May last. Witness's description of her daughter corresponded with that of the deceased. Witness said when she last saw her daughter, in Queen's Road, Chelsae, the latter tried to elude her, and when questioned said she was ashamed of herself. They were afterwards together for several hours, her daughter leaving her without stating her destination. Turks Row was close to where they met. Witness identified a piece of check ulster produced, in which some of the remains were found, as part of a garment her daughter was wearing when she last saw her. Her daughter said she expected to become a mother in September, and that the father of the child was a stonemason named Jack Fairclough, with whom she cohabited at Ipswich. She said that the man and herself came from Ipswich to Poplar, and subsequently to Battersea, where he left her, promising to return. That was on the 27th May. He had not returned. Her daughter had been in service in Chelsea, and had a scar on the wrist, caused by a broken vase.

Mary Jackson, domestic servant, and daughter of the last witness, corroborated, adding that her sister, when she met her at West Brompton, said she was not then living with anyone and had been out all night. She complained of Fairclough ill-treating her.

Dr. Kempster deposed to finding a scar on the wrist.

After other evidence, the trial was adjourned, the coroner remarking that he would make an order for the burial of a person named Elizabeth Jackson.

Leicester Daily Mercury - Thursday 04 July 1889

THE THAMES MYSTERY.

The inquest on the remains of the woman supposed to be Eliza Jackson, found in various parts of the Thames, was resumed at Battersea to-day. Mrs. Minters, wife of a labourer, 3, Cheyne-row, Chelsea, identified pieces of the cloak she had received from Mrs. Gerards some months ago and had afterwards given to deceased. Jackson told her she had been living at Ipswich, and expected to become a mother shortly. She saw her last on May 20. - Inspector Tunbridge said Jackson had a brother, but he was unable to identify any part of the remains. - Mrs. Dwyer, common lodging-house keeper, Turk's-row, Chelsea, said deceased lodged several months with her, but had not been to the house for eight or ten weeks before the body was discovered. - Other witnesses spoke to Jackson having stated that she lived at Ipswich with a man who had left her. - Kate Gaine deposed to letting a room to John Fairclough and a woman named Lizzie from Chelsea.

Manchester Courier and Lancashire General Advertiser - Friday 05 July 1889

THE THAMES MYSTERY.

Mr. Braxton Hicks, Coroner for Mid-Surrey, yesterday morning resumed his inquiry, at the Star and Garter, Battersea, upon the remains of a female which were recently found in Battersea Park, on the Chelsea Embankment, and in different parts of the Thames. The body is believed to be that of Elizabeth Jackson, a single woman, aged 24, late of 14, Turk's-row. Chelsea.

Inspectors Tonbridge and Moore, of Scotland-yard, appeared on behalf of the police.

Margaret Minter, wife of a general labourer, living at 3, Cheyne-row, Chelsea, and working at a laundry, said that about three months ago she received an ulster from Madame Givards. The fragments before her were portions of the same ulster. There was one button missing, which had been torn off by a child of hers. The button before her was the one remaining upon the ulster when she gave it away. She never wore the ulster, but gave it to Elizabeth Jackson two months ago. She knew Jackson for two and a half years as a servant. She had never seen Jackson in company with any man. Twelve months ago, Jackson called at witness's house, and told her she had left her situation, and was going into another. Then Jackson gave one of the children 1d. to buy some sweets, and, when the child returned, she said, "There's a man leaning against the kitchen window." Jackson said, "It's only my young man." About two months ago she saw Jackson, and she tried to avoid witness, because she was dressed so shabbily. But witness and her sister spoke to Jackson and asked her why she was looking so bad, and she replied that she had been living with a man in Ipswich for several months. Witness noticed Jackson's condition. Jackson said she was starving, and witness gave her 3d. and told her to call next day about dinner time. When she did call, witness noticed that she was wearing a brown skirt, similar to the one produced. Jackson said she had been living with a man who was very unkind to her, and had gone away and left her. Witness told her she had better go into the union, but Jackson said she did not like doing so, because her father and mother were in the house, and she did not want them to know the condition she was in. That night Jackson slept on the Embankment, and next day again saw the witness and had a "bit of something to eat." Then witness gave her the ulster - that was on May 20 - and the next day was the last time she saw Jackson.

By the Coroner: My husband has been out of work for two months. I have three children; and when I can get work I can earn 2s. 6d. a day.

An Inspector of Police, in reply to the Coroner, said the witness was a hard-working washerwoman.

Inspector Tonbridge stated that the woman Jackson had a brother who was a crossing-sweeper near the Consumption Hospital, Brompton; but he bad nothing to say, and had not seen his sister for several months.

Johanna Keefe, single woman, residing at 3, Cheyne-row, sister to the last witness, knew the deceased woman Elizabeth Jackson. She corroborated the evidence given by the last witness. She gave Jackson, on one occasion, some black thread to sew some tape on her clothing.

The Coroner: Look at the clothing before you, and tell me what the tape is sewn on with.

Witness: I don't like to touch them, sir.

A constable showed the witness where the tape was sewn, and the cotton was black.

Witness: The deceased, Jackson, had golden hair. One morning I saw her biting her nails, and said, "Lizzie, you'll spoil your fingers, biting them like that, and you've got genteel hands." She told witness that sometimes she slept out of doors, and at other times in lodging-houses. She was a nice-looking girl. On the 20th May Jackson sold the ticket of a counterpane to a woman in the house for 6d.

Anne Dwyer, married woman, whose husband is a labourer, rented a lodging-house at 14, Turk's-row. She had rented the house for nearly two years, and there was room for 20 lodgers. There were two rooms registered for married couples. Next door was another registered lodging-house. She knew Jackson for 20 months, and she occasionally used witness's lodging-house. Three or four weeks before the remains were found in the river she remembered seeing Jackson. She had never seen deceased in the company of any man. The ulster produced she recognised as belonging to Jackson. This was an old one worn by deceased before the other ulster mentioned was given her. Fragments of both ulsters were found with the remains.

Jenny Lees, who lodged at the house of the last witness in Turk's-row, had known the deceased for two years.

On the night of June 3 she saw the deceased with a man about nine in the evening. The man she supposed to be a navvy. He wore dark brown moleskin trousers, a peaked cloth cap, and a dark cloth coat; and his height was about 5 feet 7 or 8 inches. She was wearing at the time a check ulster like the one produced, and a brown linsey skirt, which witness also recognised.

Elizabeth Pomeroy, single, living at 14, Turk's-row, Chelsea, said she had known Elizabeth Jackson for four years. She was a servant then. On June 3 she saw her for the last time. Jackson left the brown check ulster produced in the kitchen on May 31. Seeing her afterwards, witness told her about the ulster, and [???] [???] witness to keep it and make it into a [???] [???]. When she heard about Jackson being murdered, witness did not make any use of the ulster, [???] [???] Jackson with a man on the evening of June 3, [???] description corresponding with that given by the previous witness.

Kate Paine, a married woman, whose husband is a dock labourer, said she resided at Millwall. On April 18th she remembered a man and woman coming to her door and asking for lodgings. She did let a room, for which they were to pay 4s. The man said his name was John Fairclough, and the woman was his wife. The female wore a brass ring on one finger, and she said her name was Lizzie, that she had friends in Chelsea, and a sister Kensington.

They only had a small linen bag with them and a cardboard box, which had needles and thread in it. The man left on the 28th and the woman next morning; they left her 6s. in debt. She did not see the woman the worse for drink; and the man treated her badly - roughly. When the woman went away she said she was going to try to find the man. As soon as the woman had left witness missed a counterpane, which she recognised as the one produced, and she also missed an ulster, which she had not since seen. The description of the man was as follows:- Name, John Fairclough, alias Jack Smith, 37 years of age, 5ft. 9in. in height, fair complexion, clean shaved, slightly pock-pitted; and deaf; nose twisted, broad shoulders, marks on the back of left hand. When last seen he was wearing a light green and black-striped jacket, light striped trousers, with a piece of light check let in at the back in the waist, worn over a darker pair; blue and white striped Oxford shirt, new sleeves, white muffler, lace boots, light grey or mouse-colour felt hat, and a cap of light material, usually carried in his pocket. A miller and millstone dresser. A native of Cambridgeshire; and was discharged from the 3rd Battalion Grenadier Guards on April 19, 1837. When out of work this man was accustomed to peddling brooches.

The Coroner called the attention of the jury to the fact that the evidence tended to confirm that previously given - that the deceased was Elizabeth Jackson. The police were anxious to have time for making further inquiries about the man Fairclough, and therefore should adjourn the inquiry to the 25th inst.

Lloyd's Weekly Newspaper - Sunday 07 July 1889

THE THAMES MYSTERY. FAIRCLOUGH TRACED IN LONDON.

A few days ago a stranger arrived at the village of Tipton St. John, Devonshire. He gave the name of John Fairclough, and said he came from London. As the man closely answered the description circulated by the Metropolitan police of Fairclough, the paramour of Elizabeth Jackson, the victim of the last Thames tragedy, Serjeant Pope, Devon force, communicated with Scotland-yard, and Inspector Tunbridge, of the Criminal Investigation department, who has from the first had charge of the case, proceeded on Friday to Tipton St. John. Fairclough expressed himself as perfectly willing to proceed to London, and to give any information that laid in his power. He stated that he became acquainted with Jackson last August, but he heard nothing about her death, as he is an illiterate man and very deaf. He voluntarily accompanied Inspector Tunbridge to London, and will give evidence at the adjourned inquest on Monday next. There is no charge against Fairclough, and of course he is not in custody. It is not expected that he will be able to throw much light upon the mystery.

Western Daily Press - Tuesday 09 July 1889

THE THAMES MYSTERY.
RESUMED INQUEST.

The inquest was resumed at Battersea yesterday as to the death of Elizabeth Jackson, whose mutilated remains were found in various parts of the Thames early last month. In opening the proceedings, the Coroner commented at some length on the fact of the discovery of the paramour of deceased having been announced by the press, and he complained that all through the case the evidence had been anticipated by the newspapers.

John Faircloth, in answer to the Coroner, then said was a millstone dresser, of no fixed abode. He spoke of becoming acquainted with the deceased towards the end of last September, after she had been living with a man whom she called “Charlie.” She afterwards accompanied witness to parts of the country, subsequently returning to London and staying at Millwall until the 28th of April last. On that day he left with the intention of going to Croydon, but the deceased would not accompany him. She said she would go to her mother. Witness did not leave her any money, he had none. Witness then detailed his travels in the country, eventually arriving at Ottery St. Mary, Devon, last Wednesday. There he was met by Detective Inspector Tonbridge, who brought him to London. He had heard nothing of the remains being discovered. He identified the skirt produced as having been worn by the deceased, but could not recognise the ulster. At this stage the inquiry was adjourned until the 25th inst.

Exeter Flying Post - Tuesday 09 July 1889

THE THAMES MYSTERY.

The Battersea coroner yesterday afternoon resumed his inquest touching the death of the woman Lizzie Jackson. John Fairclough, the man who lived with the deceased for several months, said he last saw her at Millwall at the end of April. He identified a linsey skirt as having belonged to Jackson, whom he described as a woman of fair complexion. When he left her in April she was pregnant, and talked about going to stay with friends at Chelsea during her confinement. She several times said she would “shunt” the child before it was born. He told her to do no such thing.

Portsmouth Evening News - Tuesday 09 July 1889

THE THAMES MYSTERY.
FAIRCLOUGH'S EVIDENCE.

Yesterday Mr. Braxton Hicks, the Mid Surrey Coroner, resumed the inquiry into the circumstances attending the death of Elizabeth Jackson, aged 24, whose mutilated remains were found in various parts of the Thames, on the Embankment, and in Battersea-park.

John Fairclough was called. He was well dressed in some clothes he had had given him, and bore the appearance of a respectable mechanic. Though uneducated, he evinced marked intelligence, promptly answering all the questions put to him. He said that he was a millstone dresser by trade, a native of March, Cambridgeshire, and 36 years of age. He first made the acquaintance of Elizabeth Jackson about the end of last November, when he met her at a public-house at the corner of Turk's-row, Chelsea, and she then told him that she had been living with a man named Charlie. He remembered it was on a Sunday night, and on the following day she agreed to go with him to Ipswich, which she did, and he was employed there for four months. She was a sober woman, and they only quarrelled now and then. On March 30th they left Ipswich and took the train to Colchester, whence they tramped to London, where they stayed for five days at a lodging-house in Whitechapel. They afterwards took lodgings at Mrs. Paine's, in Millwall. He then asked her to go with him to Croydon, but she refused, saying she would rather go to her mother at Chelsea until after her confinement. He then went Croydon alone, having no money to leave her, and got a few days' work at Waddon Flour Mills. From there he went to Wandsworth, sleeping two nights "near the railway," then tramped to Isleworth, Uxbridge, Ware, Bishop's Stortford, Saffron Walden, Cambridgeshire, St. Ives, Huntingdon, St. Neots, Biggleswade (staying the Red Lion), Hitchin, Luton, and St. Alban's, and reached Harpenden on May 31. He also went to Watford, where he slept at the Red Lion, kept by an Army pensioner named Sullivan, and on June 3 (the last day deceased was seen alive) he was at High Wycombe, and called at Great Marlow on his way to Reading, where he stayed two nights. He subsequently visited Oldham, where he was bitten by a dog, and had the wound cauterised by the parish doctor. On Whit-Sunday he visited Basingstoke, and continued travelling westward until he reached Tipton, near Ottery St. Mary, where the police found him on Saturday. From the time he left Jackson at Millwall he had neither seen nor heard anything of her. He had not read the newspapers - in fact, had hardly seen one in the parts he visited, and had consequently not heard of a body having been found in the Thames. He knew of no one who would have been likely to have done deceased an injury. He did not hear her mention the address of any house to which she was likely to go in Battersea. The linsey dress produced he had bought for her in Ipswich.

By the Jury: Deceased was eight months advanced in pregnancy when he left her.

Inspector Tunbridge, who had travelled down to Tipton St. John on receipt of a communication from Sergeant Pope, of the Devonshire Constabulary, stated that when he found Fairclough at Ottery St. Mary he was wearing the same clothes described by Mrs. Paine as those worn when left her, and the Inspector added that inquiries had already been set on foot with a view to verify the dates and places mentioned by Fairclough, and that it had been ascertained that he was at Croydon on the day he had stated.

The Coroner then stated that that was as far as he could now carry the case. The police had been so very successful in procuring the identification of the woman that they might yet be able bring out other facts, and with that view he would adjourn the inquiry until the date originally fixed - viz., the 25th inst.

Whitstable Times and Herne Bay Herald - Saturday 13 July 1889

THE THAMES MYSTERY.

Mr. A. Braxton Hicks resumed his inquiry on Thursday at Battersea, into the circumstances attending the death of Elizabeth Jackson, aged 24 years, a single woman, late of Chelsea, whose mutilated remains were found in the Thames, in Battersea Park, and in a garden on the Chelsea Embankment in the early part of last month. - Margaret Minter, a married woman, said that about three months ago she received an ulster from a Madame Gerards, for whom she did laundry work. She was certain that the piece of material produced belonged to the same ulster. After keeping it a month the gave it to the deceased Lizzie Jackson, whom she had known about two-and-a-half years as a domestic servant - In reply to the coroner, Inspector Tunbridge said that the deceased had a brother, who was not satisfied with her identification, but merely went by the condition of her hands. - Johanna Keefe, sister to Mrs. Minter, also identified other portions of deceased's clothing. The deceased used to bite her nails very much, and on the last occasion that witness saw her she took her hand away from her mouth. When she washed herself witness remarked what a nice genteel hand she had and what a pity it was she bit her nails. She laughed, and replied, "They will be more genteel shortly." She said that sometimes she slept out of doors in the open air and sometimes in lodging-houses. - Jennie Lee said she had known the deceased about two years. She believed she was in a situation down to the time that she went to

Ipswich. For the last seven months the deceased had led a loose life. About two months ago she returned to Turks-row, and then said that her man had left her the day before, and she had no home nor anything to do. She had seen her with different men, but no one in particular. - Elizabeth Pomeroy said she had known Lizzie Jackson four years, at time she was in service. She last saw her on the 31st of May, and that same day she found the ulster produced hanging in kitchen. On the 3rd of June she and Jennie Lee met the deceased outside the Royal Hospital Tavern with a man dressed like a workman. Witness said to her "I suppose you're going to Battersea," and she said, "That's just where I am going." She was quite sober at that time. The man had a little bit of whiskers. He was wearing a heavy pilot jacket, and looked like a navvy. - Kate Paine, of Poplar, deposed to the deceased and Faircloth lodging at her house. The woman said she had friends living at Chelsea and Kensington. During the time they were together witness did not see the man beat her, but he seemed to treat her very roughly. Deceased told witness he had beaten her, and that she was a month advanced in pregnancy. Faircloth did no work while with them, but said he had been down to the millstone works to try and get work. - The inquiry was then adjourned until the 25th inst, in order that Faircloth and the man who was last seen with deceased should attend the court.

Portsmouth Evening News - Thursday 18 July 1889

The Thames Mystery.

There is said to no connection between the Thames mystery case and the Whitechapel series of murders. It is true that letters have been received by the police threatening fresh murders, and similar communications have been addressed to the office of The Daily Telegraph during the past few weeks, in which the writer disclaimed any connection with the Thames murder and spoke of deeds yet to be done. Not much importance has been attached to these productions.

Exeter Flying Post - Thursday 25 July 1889

THE THAMES MYSTERY.

The adjourned inquest on the remains supposed to be those of Elizabeth Jackson, late of Turk's-row, Chelsea, found in a mutilated condition at Battersea and Chelsea, was held to-day at Battersea. Inspector Tunbridge detailed the result of the investigations of the police, and said it had been clearly demonstrated that the man Fairclough, with whom the deceased had lived, had not been near London for several days before and after the woman was killed. The head and some of the internal organs had not been discovered, though the river had been dragged and an exhaustive search made in the locality of Chelsea and Battersea. The Coroner having addressed the jury, they found that the body was that of Elizabeth Jackson and that she had been murdered by some person or persons unknown. They highly commended the conduct of the police engaged in the investigation.

Reynolds's Newspaper - Sunday 28 July 1889

THE THAMES MYSTERY.

Mr. A. Braxton Hicks, the Mid-Surrey coroner, resumed his inquiry at the Sat and Garter, Church-road, Battersea, into the circumstances attending the death of Elizabeth Jackson, aged twenty-four years, a single woman, late of 14 Turk's-row, Chelsea, whose mutilated remains – minus the head and certain of the internal organs – were found in various parts of the Thames, a shrubbery in Battersea-park, and in a garden on the Chelsea-embankment, on June 14th and subsequent days.

FAIRCLOTH'S INNOCENCE UNDOUBTED

Inspector Tunbridge again appeared to watch the case on behalf of the Criminal Investigation Department, and being called by the coroner he explained the action of the police in connection with the matter. All the important parts of the body had, said the inspector, been found except the head. Since Faircloth had given evidence before the coroner, Inspector Moore and Sergeant Turrell had been over the route indicated by him as having been pursued by him. The officers had visited Biggleswade, Bishop's Sortford, Hitchin, High Wycombe, St. Albans, Great Marlow, Reading, Odiham, and other places. On the night of the 3rd of June, it was satisfactorily shown that he was stopping at High Wycombe, at the Goat public-house, and on the previous nights at Watford. He was traced to all the places he had named, and at all of them he had been calling at mills, trying to get employment; and the police had further quite satisfied themselves that during all that time he had never been in London or had the opportunity of coming to London – that was to say, for ten days before and ten days after the death of Elizabeth Jackson. Throughout the whole of the time he had been wearing the conspicuous striped jacket he went away with, and going about in his own name. The Thames had been dragged both above and below the Albert-bridge for the purpose of finding the head; the ornamental waters of Battersea-park and the shrubberies had also been searched, and inquiries had been made of dustmen and others, but without result. Every suggestion thrown out by the public and the press had also been followed out where practicable; in fact, the police had travelled through many counties, and had spent a great amount of time upon the matter, but without any result.

THE GARMENT MARKED "FISHER."

In consequence of the statement made by Faircloth as to the purchase of the article of underclothing which bore the name of "Fisher," he (the inspector) proceeded to Lowestoft, where he traced out a domestic servant named Lucy Elizabeth Fisher, who at once identified the garment as having once belonged to her. The garment was one of several she had made five years ago, and had been marked in marking-ink by her father, who was traced to Bill Quay, on the Tyne, below Newcastle, and who identified the writing. There was also found the mother of Fisher at Byker, near Newcastle, who stated that she had sold the article among other old rags at Lowestoft about the period Faircloth mentioned when he said he bought it at a lodging-house. This completed the identity of every portion of clothing which had been found in conjunction with the body.

"MURDERED BY A PERSON UNKNOWN."

After a few moments' deliberation, the jury found that the body was that of Elizabeth Jackson, and that she was wilfully murdered by some person or persons unknown, adding their expression of opinion that the greatest credit was due to the police for the vigilance and activity they had shown in the case.

CASE 4
The Pinchin Street Murder
September 1889

Sunderland Daily Echo and Shipping Gazette - Tuesday 10 September 1889

ANOTHER HORROR IN WHITECHAPEL.
"JACK THE RIPPER" AGAIN.
THE HEAD AND LIMBS MISSING.
THE VICTIM UNIDENTIFIED
NO TRACE OF THE MURDERER.

The Press Association learns that a woman has been found murdered and mutilated under circumstances similar to those attending previous outrages in the same locality, in Back Church-lane, Whitechapel.

The Central News announces another "Jack-the-Ripper" murder - the worst of the series. It says about half-past five o'clock this morning the policeman on beat in the Cable-street end of Back Church-lane - a wide, but at night, very dark and dangerous thoroughfare in St George's in the East - made a horrible discovery under one of the huge railway arches which are situated off Cable-street. About twenty yards to the right, in a dark corner in the main railway arch, he found the body of a woman which had been mutilated in a fearful manner. The arms and head were completely severed from the body, and were removed by the murderer. This must have been done with a very sharp knife and by the aid of other instruments, as the mutilation was done in a by no means clumsy manner, but showed considerable surgical skill. She was also terribly mutilated about the abdomen in way which has characterised nearly all the series of Whitechapel murders which are identified with "Jack-the-Ripper." The policeman immediately whistled for assistance, and in very short time a sergeant and some constables were on the spot. The scene of the murder was quickly surrounded, and every corner and alley the district, but nothing whatever could be seen which afforded any clue to the whereabouts of the author or authors of the diabolical outrage. As soon as the news of the murder was communicated at Leman-street Police Station, which is only about three minutes' walk from Back Church-lane, the inspector in charge communicated with Scotland Yard, and detectives were immediately sent down. Chief Commissioner Monro was also informed, and he, along with a number of Scotland Yard officers, came down and visited the place and the whole locality around Cable-street. Before the body was removed to St George's-in-the-East Mortuary, Phillips made examination of it, and the Central News learns that he, as well as the Scotland Yard authorities, are distinctly of opinion that this is very far the worst of the series of horrible tragedies which have occurred in the East End of London during the past 18 months. They are inclined to attribute the committal of this murder to the unknown fiend whose handiwork can be clearly traced throughout the preceding barbarities. The news of the murder spread rapidly throughout the courts and alleys of Cable-street, and large crowds had gathered in front of the railway arch before six o'clock in the morning. The scene of the murder is a peculiarly quiet and dark one, and just the place where such a deed could be committed without much fear of interruption.

A Policeman Close Hand.

The policeman on beat was doing his rounds only about 20 yards distant. This is, of course, presuming that the murder was actually committed where the body was found. The arch, strictly speaking, is Pinchin-street, which extends from Back Church-street to Christian-street, and runs parallel with Cable-street. The body was removed to St George's-in-the-East Mortuary, where it now lies awaiting identification.

Must Have Taken an Hour.

The archway is wide, and carts and barrows lie in various positions along the walls. There is, however, only one exit, and this by Back Church-lane. This, however, leads directly into Cable-street, and thence by numerous ways into Leman-street and the scene of the other East End murders. From the close inspection of the various mutilations it is thought that the deed must have taken over an hour to accomplish, and all this time a policeman was on duty not far off.

The Victim.

The victim appears to have been a rather short stout woman, 30 years of age, of dark complexion, and rather shabbily dressed. From appearance she seems to have led a dissipated existence, as the body is but poorly nourished, and she must have been a hard drinker.

Several women have visited the mortuary, but to the present the body has not been identified.

Another Unfortunate.

The woman is believed have been a prostitute. Her arms and head were completely severed from the body, and she was fearfully disembowelled.

ANOTHER MYSTERY.

It seems very hard to believe that the murderer could have escaped the notice both of the police and the detectives, who are swarming the neighbourhood. Yet this, the most horrible of all the series, as far as present clues go, seems almost certain to develop into another East End mystery.

THE CLUE TO IDENTITY.

Identification, under the circumstances, will be very difficult, the main clue of course being the woman's clothing, which corresponds to that generally worn by the poorer class of women in Whitechapel. Crowds continue to gather in Pinchin-street and Back Church-lane, and more interest and indignation has been excited regarding this murder than in the one in Castle-alley, which took place about two months ago.

BAFFLED.

The police are again completely baffled. Instead of assuming a more cautious and watchful attitude, the murderer seems to have been emboldened by his success, and it seems very strange that no suspicions whatever were aroused by the appearance of a man walking along this neighbourhood, and at this early hour of the morning, with such a bulky parcel as must have been used in conveying away the arms and head of the murdered woman.

ANOTHER ACCOUNT.

The Press Association says:- At an early hour this morning the inhabitants of Whitechapel were thrown into a state of wild excitement by a rumour to the effect that the notorious criminal known as "Jack the Ripper" had again been at his work in their midst. It was about six o'clock this morning when news first became noised abroad, and within half an hour of the time a great and excited crowd had collected in the neighbourhood of Pinchin-street, St. George's, the locality in which the tragedy was said to have been committed, and which lies in close proximity to the scene of outrages which have given Whitechapel its evil reputation. From inquiries made by the Press Association reporters, it appears that while a murder has undoubtedly been committed there is, so far as at present can be ascertained, no resemblance to those which have previously been perpetrated.

A constable on his beat in Pinchin-street, which lies between Commercial-road and Lemon-street, noticed something in a sack lying beneath one of the arches of the London, Tilbury, and Southend Railway. The sack appeared to have been deposited just at the mouth of the archway, which is partially protected by some fencing, but not such as to offer any obstruction to a person desiring to enter. On opening the sack the officer found that it contained the body of a woman, minus the head, legs, and arms. There was no blood about the place, and the trunk appeared to have been brought from elsewhere. The constable despatched a messenger for ambulance, and the body was conveyed to St George's Mortuary, Cable-street, where it lies awaiting a post mortem examination. The coroner, Mr Wynne Baxter, was also notified of the discovery. The police state that the woman appears to have been dead three or four days. Much of the flesh was decomposed. They are unable to say where the trunk is mutilated further than being dismembered. It is impossible to give the age of the woman, and to the present there is no clue to her identity.

Other Finds reported.

It is reported that about a quarter to nine some clothes stained with blood had been found in Hooper-street near by, and an excited crowd collected round a warehouse yard there. Some material bearing blood stains was certainly found, but whether it is connected with the mystery is only a matter of conjecture. The crowd set to work to see if they could find any trace of the missing limbs, but without any apparent result. The scene of the tragedy is a railway arch which forms part of the new Great Eastern Railway goods depot, in Bishopsgate-street.

Discovered at Daylight.

A later account says:- Shortly after five o'clock, P.C. Pannett, 237, was patrolling his beat when, by the light of breaking day, he noticed a bundle under the archway. He found it contained the body of a woman with tbe arms attached, but with the head and legs missing. It was slightly decomposed. The stomach had been cut in a brutal manner. Pannett called assistance, and in a short time Supt. Arnold and a large body of plain clothes and uniformed officers were on the spot with an ambulance and medical assistance. It was certified that the mutilated trunk was that of a woman who had been dead at least four days, but only deposited beneath the archway during the night.

Exactly a Year Ago.

Opinion is divided in the district as to whether the crime is another of the series which has made the name of "Jack the Ripper" a terror in the East End. The spot where the body was found is only a few yards from Berner-street, where exactly a year almost to a day the mutilated remains of a woman were found.

The Constable Interviewed.

A representative of the Press Association this morning had an interview with Constable Pannett. He stated that he was on duty near the railway arches in Pinchin-street, soon after five o'clock this morning, when, turning his lantern into one of the arches, he was horrified to discover the woman's body minus the head and legs. The trunk was naked with the exception of a small piece of calico or linen resembling a chemise. It appeared to have been carried in some coarse cloth or sacking. The remains were somewhat decomposed, and the woman must have been dead some time. Another policeman stated that he passed the place where the body was found a short time before, and is positive that there was nothing there then, so that it would appear that it had been carried to the spot. A visit to the mortuary shows that the abdomen is split completely up. The severed flesh is dark coloured, decomposition having set in consequent on exposure to the air.

No Blood on the Ground.

The Central News Says:- The constable on the beat, who found the remains in the railway arch Castle-street, was P.C. 239 H, Wm. Pennett. It was exactly half-past five when the morning light enabled him to see the body of a woman lying in the corner of the railway arch, and he at once realised that it was a lifeless piece of humanity. It was evident, from a closer examination, that the woman was not murdered on the spot where she was found. There was, for instance, no blood upon the ground, and very little upon the body, whereas had she been murdered in the arch there must have been ample evidence of it. The experts are of opinion that the body must have been brought to the arch, and left there between five and half-past five.

The State of the Body.

The trunk when discovered was in a completely nude state and minus the head. The legs were taken away, and not the arms as at first reported. The body was lying on the stomach, there was a clear cut from the waist downwards. A chemise was lying in a heap on the body; the garment had been cut down and was much bloodstained. No other clothing has yet been found. There is a mark round the waist as though it had been tied tightly round, and this was probably done when the body was removed. The women, according to the opinion of the doctor, must have been between 30 and 40 years of age and about 5 feet 8 inches in height. She was stoutly built and dark. Portions of the hair on the trunk are of a dark brown colour. The trunk measures 2 feet 3 inches and the arms 2 feet 2 inches. The waist measures 33 inches. There is no mark of a wedding ring on the finger, and she had never suckled a child.

The Spot Described.

The arch where the remains were found belongs to the Great Eastern Railway, and is rented by the Whitechapel Board of Works as a stone yard. There is a hoarding which has been pulled down, and the arch is therefore visible from the street.

The Doctor's Opinion.

Dr Clark is the medical officer who made the first examination, Dr Phillips being absent on his holidays in Bournemouth. In the opinion of this gentleman, the woman had been dead from two to three days when found.

No Motive in this Case.

An examination of the abdomen by Dr Phillips' assistant showed that nothing had been removed from the intestines or any other part of the stomach. The motive for crime is therefore less apparent in this case than in several which have preceded it. There was nothing by which the remains could be identified, nor anything to show whether the woman was married or single. The Scotland Yard authorities are assisting the local police, and the detective force has been increased.

No Marks.

Dr Phillips has arranged to hold a post-mortem on the remains at 3 o'clock this afternoon at the mortuary adjoining the vestry hall of St. George's-in-the-East, at

Cable-street. The inquest will probably be held to-morrow at the vestry hall, Cable-street. The body, it is stated, does not bear any marks which may lead to identification. So far as has been ascertained up to the present, there are no scars whatever upon any part.

THREE SAILORS ARRESTED.

Mr Thomas Arnold, the district Superintendent, was summoned, and took charge of the police arrangements from an early hour. Inspector Pinehorn and Inspectors Reid and Donald Swanson and Henry Moore are ably carrying out the chief's directions with a view to trace the perpetrator of the crime. One of the first things discovered by the police when a thorough search was made was three sailors sleeping in a railway arch adjoining that in which the remains were found. They were detained and closely examined at the police station, but it was evident they knew nothing of the murder or of depositing the remains on the spot. They had neither seen nor heard anything, and were accordingly discharged.

Pall Mall Gazette - Tuesday 10 September 1889

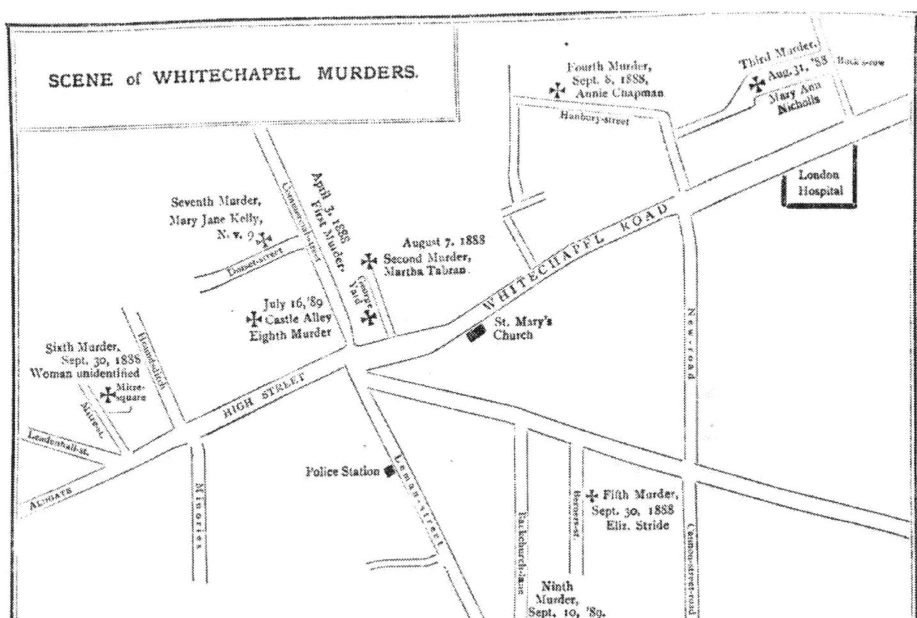

LATEST EAST-END HORROR.
A WOMAN MURDERED AND MUTILATED.
THE VICTIM'S HEAD AND ARMS CUT OFF.
THE TRUNK FOUND IN A SACK.

At an early hour this morning the inhabitants of Whitechapel were thrown into a state of wild excitement by rumour to the effect that the notorious criminal known as “Jack the Ripper” had been again at his work in their midst. It was about six o'clock this morning when the news first became noised abroad, and within half an hour of that time an excited crowd had collected in the neighbourhood of Pinchin-street, St. George’s, the locality in which the tragedy was said to have been committed, and which lies in close proximity to the scenes of the outrages which have given Whitechapel its evil reputation. From inquiries, however, it appears that while a murder has no doubt been committed, there is, so far as at present can be ascertained, nothing in the nature of the crime to connect it with the frightful murders popularly ascribed to “Jack the Ripper.”

It was at half-past five this morning when a constable in Pinchin-street - which lies between Commercial-road and Leman-street - noticed something in a sack lying beneath one of the arches of the London, Tilbury, and South-end Railway. The sack appears to have been deposited just at the mouth of the archway, partially protected by some broken fencing, which is not such as to offer any obstruction to a person desiring to enter. On opening the sack the officer found it to contain the dead body of a woman, denuded of head, legs and arms. There was no blood about the spot, and the trunk enclosed in the sack appeared to have been brought from some other place and deposited in the spot where it was discovered by the policeman. Attracting the attention of some passers by, he despatched a messenger for the ambulance, and the body was at once conveyed to the St. Georges mortuary, Cable-street, where it now lies awaiting a post-mortem examination, which, it is expected, will be conducted to-day. Mr. Coroner Baxter has been communicated with, and furnished with particulars, and an inquest is to be held in due course.

The police state that the woman appears to have been dead quite four or five clays, and that much of the flesh is putrefied. They are unable to say whether the trunk is mutilated in addition to the dismemberment already described. It is impossible to give the age of the woman, and up to the present time there is no clue to her identity.

Three arrests were made this morning, but no importance is attached to them. The men so arrested - merely on suspicion - were two sailors and a shoeblack, who were found sleeping beneath the arch, not a great distance from the body, at the time of the discovery. About a quarter to nine it was reported that some clothes stained with blood had been discovered in Hooper-street, which is near to Pinchin-street, and at once a large and excited crowd collected around a warehouse yard in the thoroughfare. Some material stained with blood appears to have been found there, but its connection with the supposed murder is at present only matter of conjecture. However, the discovery so far aroused and excited the bystanders that they at once commenced a search in the yard in the hope of finding a trace of the legs, arms, or head of the woman. They were engaged in this gruesome pursuit for some time without any result.

FURTHER PARITICULARS.

The Press Association gives the following further details - The scene of the tragedy is a roadway arch abutting on a place known as Dark-alley. There is nothing whatever to prevent a person so desirous of walking through a stoneyard which lies on the further side of the arch which forms part of the new Great Eastern Railway goods depot at Bishopsgate. It is approached by numerous dark and winding small streets from Leman-street and from the Whitechapel High-street.

Shortly after five o'clock Police-constable Pannell, 239 H, was patrolling his beat when, by the light of the breaking day, he noticed a bundle under the massive open structure. On examining it, it was found to be the trunk of the woman with the arms attached, but the head and legs are missing. It was slightly decomposed. The abdomen bore those brutal evidences of the work of Jack the Ripper which characterized the previous murders in the locality. The stomach was cut in a shocking manner. Pannell immediately summoned further assistance and within a short time Superintendent Arnold and a large body of plain clothes and uniform officers were hastening to the scene with an ambulance and medical assistance. It was certified that the mutilated trunk was that of a woman who had been dead at least four days, but only left exposed under the arch during the night. It was removed to the St. George's mortuary for the purpose of a further medical examination.

WHAT THE CONSTABLE WHO FOUND THE BODY SAYS.

One of our representatives, writing from the scene of the murder at Whitechapel at eleven o'clock says:- I have just had an interview with Constable 239 H, who found the body of Jack the Ripper's latest victim. He I said: “I was passing along Pinchin-street, at the foot of Backchurch-lane, about a quarter-past five this morning, when I saw lying on the ground the trunk of a woman, the head and legs of which had been severed and were not present. The body was quite naked, except for a piece of torn linen which might have been a shift or portion of a pair of drawers, thrown over it. The body was fearfully disembowelled, and was marked as if it had been carried in a sack. My own opinion is that it had been so conveyed to the spot where I found it. The stench was something terrific. It would have been impossible to have passed it.”

Another constable of the H division said:- "I heard the whistle of 239 H, and hurried to the spot and saw the body just as he has described it. There was absolutely nothing whereby to recognize it. We sent for an ambulance, and the body was taken to the mortuary of St. George's Vestry."

"JACK THE RIPPER'S" NINTH VICTIM?

If, as is suggested with some show of reason, the gruesome discovery of this morning is also to be attributed to the perpetrator of the atrocities commonly associated with the name of "Jack the Ripper," this latest murder will be, as the accompanying plan shows, the ninth murder of the series.

A STRANGE COINCIDENCE.

It is a somewhat remarkable fact that one of the horrible Whitechapel murders of last year took place on September the 8th. Consequently, the revolting Backchurch-lane crime must have been in perpetration at a time only a few hours removed from the exact anniversary of a previous atrocity.

Pall Mall Gazette - Wednesday 11 September 1889

MURDER MORNING IN WHITECHAPEL.

There can be no doubt about it. The East-ender is blase of murders. This was certainly the feeling in the East-end yesterday. When we started for the scene of the murder the West was just awakening, but the news was printed as early as half-past nine, and selling like wildfire all along the Underground line. The City clerk invested another penny in another paper, and his master was not behind him in curiosity. The newsboys were blowing out their little lungs with the news. But once in the Commercial-road, roaring with traffic, Jack the Ripper was lost in the crowd. “Good morning. Another murder!” “Oh! how many’s that? Good morning.” The carmen and the hawkers and the shopkeepers are too busy to dally with drams of gossip.

On the way to the scene of the murder we walked down Leman-street. Two policemen were sunning themselves at the door of the station, and smiling, for it was a pleasant morning even in the environs of Whitechapel. On the walls was a Murder notice printed in big, staring letters; through the door you could see a squad of policemen drilling in the yard. These were the signs of official activity. The police drill, and plaster London with Murder notices. As usual, the officials at the door “know’d nothing. They ‘ad ‘eard that somethink ‘ad bin found.” And we left the two gentlemen still sunning themselves and brushing the flies off their noses. We passed on and turned into Cable-street, which is a narrow, filthy road, blocked up with barrows of vegetables, fish, and butcher’s meat. The housewives of Whitechapel were evidently not much affected by the news. Meat had risen a farthing, which was a much more serious matter. With more violence than was quite chivalrous we urged our way onwards through the chaffering housekeepers, stumbling through the autumnal cabbage leaves which lay thick on the ground as our old friends of Vallombrosa. It was evident that marketing was more interesting than murdering. Did we see howling mobs of women, with arms akimbo and faces aflame with rage? No. The smells were strong, the language was strong, and there was a high-flavoured tone about Cable-street; but of horror or consternation not a bit. "They've got another job, and really, sir, if you just cast your eyes around, you will see that a murder more or less is not worth mentioning. It's good for you newspaper reporters. And for good liars, sir, give me a newspaper reporter, especially the seedy ones who are always lifting their elbows in the bars. You see I have come down in the world. I, too, gentlemen, was once connected with the Press. It is a dangerous profession. May you be morning or evening? It's those evening extra-special specials that take the cake, vulgarly speaking. Munchausens, gentlemen, Munchausens. Now as for this miserable trunk that you are down here about - lemons, I see you're drinking mild drink, sir, you like it mild? -excuse the interruption - well you have given me this drink, or I *should* put it in the past tense, for you see sir my glass is - thank you, your health, well, as I say, I like to earn my wages - this trunk which is making all this fuss - this headless, legless trunk - why, it is a week old - only a stale trunk." When we had explored the horrible nest of tortuous slums, in the centre of which the body-carrier had deposited his load, it was evident that our casual acquaintance, who had picked us up at the cats' meat shop at the corner of Backchurch-lane, was perfectly correct when he said that you "might do a murder a minute, send a large family to the Board school, and die a natural death." The whole neighbourbood is a network of slums which it would be impossible to examine, and every slum has an outlet, with runs like a rabbit warren.

Cable-street runs at right angles to Leman-street, and Backchurch-lane runs off Cable-street at an angle of forty-five degrees. It is a murderous-looking neighbourhood when the September sun is shining, and the street is alive with hucksters and housewives. At night it might be called Murderer's Mansions. The entrance to the "Lane" is bridged over for the railway, and it is under one of fifty gloomy arches along which the line runs that the human trunk with its covering of coarse sacking was found. Each arch would conceal a body, or hide a murderer. These arches form one side of Pinchin-street, at right angles to which run rows of brick cottages. On the doorstep of one of these a dirty woman was sitting with her elbows on her knees and her chin resting on her hands. Through the passage we caught sight of a naked boy performing his ablutions at the pump in the back-yard.

"Another murder. Who was it?"

"No one knows, sir. No head, no nothink."

"Do you feel nervous?"

"This is a lonely place of a dark night."

"But you have gas-lamps and policemen."

"A gas-lamp, yes. But police we don't see for hours, as often as not."

It is pathetic to see the love for flowers and leaves which these miserables show. One side of the street was a mass of creepers, thick with dust and filth, but still things with leaves. The East-end creeper is a kindly parasite, which clothes the grimiest of walls, and even serves for a window-blind.

You may be quite certain there were lots of police about just now. We tackled one with a beery face, but he only leered.

"D-- it all, you don't expect us to identify a trunk without a 'ead, do you?" remarked his companion.

Then we walked back to the fatal arch, which was guarded by three jovial bobbies, who kept a crowd of fifty drunken, lazy sluts and children, and an old coalheaver or two quiet.

"Where was it found?" we asked one of the guards.

"Here. Just where you see the pink dust. It's carbolic."

"To cover the blood?"

"Blood – there weren't no blood. It stunk. Move on, please."

In the middle of the road a sandy female, without a covering on her head, was addressing the crowd. We took the liberty of joining in the conversation.

"Somebody missing, missus?"

"Ay, guv'nor. A sort of relation of mine. A respectable woman, not an unfortunate. Oh! No. Quite respectable, and you may say she was born in the neighbourhood. She has not been seen since yesterday morning, and we think it's her. If you call at No. ---street, you can find out for you'self."

The house was closed, but we dropped in to have another "small lemon" at the "pub" to pursue enquiries. The bar was filled with five giantesses drinking ale, but the murder was never mentioned. We left the ladies and called in at a little shop, where we found that the missing washerwoman's son had been down to "the house" and found his mother there. She'd only been on the drink, and had gone to the House to sleep it off. She was quite a respectable woman, they all told us – a most respect'ble body; but when she had a bit o' drink inside her – well, no doubt she might have gone along of "Jack" then. Indeed, everyone seemed to have only two ideas on the subject: first, that another murder was the most natural thing in the world; and secondly, that it would also have been the most natural thing in the world to have "gone along of Jack." And as we turned round for a lst look at the sordid squalor of the houses and streets, we were of the same opinion also. “Another murder.” “Of course, why not?”

Whitechapel is becoming so blase with murder that yesterday’s occurrence hardly caused a ripple of emotion in the East-end murder-land. Incredible as it would have seemed a short time ago, it is by no means improbable that before long a couple of lines at the bottom of a column will be all that is deemed necessary by the newspapers to record the discovery of another victim of Jack the Ripper. The newspapers do not think it worth while to chronicle the discovery of dead babies, which are picked up almost every day in various parts of London; and unless something is done to change the character of the victim, the death and mutilation of another poor woman in Whitechapel are things which are already gravitating to the level of infanticide - that is to say, they are becoming one of the ordinary normal incidents of our very complex civilization.

So far as can be judged from the surgical examination of the remains found down Whitechapel way, the murdered woman has fallen a prey, not to Jack the Ripper, who always kills *in situ*, apparently for a certain specific object, but to a murderer who obviously committed his crime at a place other than that where the body was found, and the interior of the trunk is said to be intact. It seems therefore that there are two murderers: one Jack the Ripper who kills on the spot and the other the person who cuts his victims up into fragments and distributes their remains about the metropolis. If this theory be correct, Jack the Ripper should only be credited with eight murders, while the other, as yet unnamed mutilator, has down to his gory score the murder of the women whose remains were found at Whitehall, Battersea, and Backchurch-lane.

THE WHITECHAPEL TRAGEDY.
WHO IS THE MURDERER?
A CURIOUS DREAM.
EVIDENCE AT THE INQUEST TO-DAY.

There is little or nothing new to report this morning in connection with the horrible discovery in Whitechapel yesterday. A correspondent sends us the following curious statement about his theory of the murder:- "I dreamed on Sunday night that I saw a man whom I know well, and have suspected for some time, killing a woman. The dream was so vivid that I mentioned it next morning to my friend. Hence I was not surprised when to-day the body of the latest victim was discovered. The detectives are devoting their efforts and the skill they possess mainly to the tracking of this very man with reference to whom information was communicated to them shortly after the murder of Mary Kelly in Miller's-court, Dorset-street, on the 9th November last year. That information included an array of facts and circumstances relating to the individual suspected, which pointed more strongly to his being 'Jack the Ripper' than any of the many persons who have been arrested or 'shadowed' by the police. Since the end of

November the detectives have tried in every conceivable way to trace the whereabouts of this 'suspect,' but without success. He was seen in the East-end immediately after the Berner-street and Mitre-square murders not long before the Miller's-court tragedy, and also, it is stated on reliable authority, the Saturday evening preceding the Castle-alley deed, and then within a stone's throw of that place.

"The murderer is supposed by the most experienced detectives to be a man calculated not to attract special notice, and who is so cautious and artful that he can guard himself against suspicion. Though not a muscular specimen of humanity, he is not of slim build. He is between twenty-eight and thirty years of age, about five feet six in height, and is somewhat round-shouldered. His forehead is low, but extremely broad and smooth his hair is black; his complexion sallow. His eyes, perhaps, form the most distinctive feature about him. They are of a deep brown colour, and large for the size of the face in which they are set. Though they usually betoken determination and firmness, they sometimes soften to even a girl's tenderness of expression. He wears no beard: Like his hair, his moustache is black, and though heavy and full-grown, it fails to hide a mouth garnished by rows of pearly white teeth, because they are revealed by his thick lower lip, which hangs somewhat loosely.

"This suspect knows the East-end intimately, and stayed for some considerable time in Spitalfields, in close proximity to the Columbia Meat Market. He was born in England, but is of Jewish parentage. The peculiar features, however, which commonly characterize the Hebrew race are not so clearly stamped in his face as in the case of the average Jew. He is a man of culture, and one of his favourite pursuits is said to be the study of anatomy, of which, theoretically speaking, he has as extensive a knowledge as the average surgeon. He is of somewhat eccentric habits. He has a great dislike of the opposite sex, avoiding the company of females. He has also made low life in London a special study. It used to be a hobby of his to get himself up in all sorts of disguises - and in this he was an adept - and explore the most notorious parts of the East-end, particularly Spitalfields and Whitechapel, visiting the low public-houses, mixing with all and sundry, and frequently spending the night in common lodging-houses, in order to see for himself the routine of the 'dosser's' life. It is not at all likely that he would appear in Whitechapel in the ordinary dress he used to wear, which consisted of a black diagonal coat, with vest to match, dark tweed trousers, and either a hard or soft felt hat."

THE INQUEST ON THE REMAINS.

At the Vestry Hall of St. George's-in-the-East, at ten o'clock this morning, before Mr. Wynne E. Baxter, the coroner for the south-eastern district, and a jury there was held an inquiry into the circumstances attending the discovery of the remains.

The first witness was Constable William Pennett, who said he went on duty on Monday night at ten o'clock, that he saw nothing of an unusual nature while on his beat, which engaged him for half an hour. He passed along: Pinchin-street once, entering by Christian-street and walking to Backchurch-lane, occasionally turning down Frederick street, a dark lane under the railway arches at the back of Pinchin-street. At about twenty-five minutes past five in the morning, coming from Christian-street along Pinchin-street on the side opposite the arch, his attention was attracted by seeing under the arch what he thought to be a bundle. It was lying about 4½ or 5 yards from the mouth of the archway. He found on approaching it that it was not a bundle, but the remains of a human body, with only two or three pieces of rag upon it. The head had been taken from the body, and the legs were missing. The shoulders lay towards Backchurch-lane. There were no marks of footprints, and he saw no drops of blood about. He waited a minute or two before blowing his whistle as he did not want to bring a crowd. A man came by with a broom, and he asked him to "fetch my mate" The man said, "What's on, governor?" Pennett answered, "Tell him I've got a job; make haste." The man went up Backchurch-lane to the adjoining beat where Fennett's comrade was. Two constables quickly came to the spot. Witness told one of them to find the inspector as he had a dead body there. Very soon Inspector Pinhorn arrived on the scene, a search through the arches was made, and two men like sailors were found asleep in the furthest arch, and in the middle arch a shoeblack lay on the stones, but no other persons had been seen. One of the sailors had a pipe in his mouth, and it is not certain whether he was asleep. All three were taken to the station. They made no statement to the constable. "The last time," continued Pennett, "I passed the arch before I found the body was just before five o'clock. I can fix the time, because I had to call a man at five o'clock. Daylight was breaking, and had the trunk been there I should have seen it, I did not see it," While on his beat he saw no one with any bundle, nor any costermonger's cart moving. Dr. Clark, assistant to the police surgeon came on the spot about half an hour after the alarm was given, and the body was removed to the mortuary shortly after six o'clock. He did not know if the arch was often used for sleeping purposes, it being the first time he had been on that beat. In answer to a juryman Pennett said that he fancied the body must have been brought in a sack. There were no marks of a trail, but the body looked as if it had been lifted into the arch and laid down, as there was no appearance of dust or dirt on the moist portion of it. In answer to another juryman, Pennett said that he or any other constable would have at once stopped any person carrying a bundle at any hour of the night.

Inspector Charles Pinhorn, of the H Division, was then called, and corroborated Constable Pennett's evidence. He said the arrested men made statements at the police-station to the effect that when they went into the Arches (two entering at 4 A.M., the third about 2 A.M.) there was nothing in the arch, and they had heard no noise in the night. Frequently tramps and casuals try to sleep in the arches but they are always turned out. The police have no right in the arches or yard, but still all such isolated spots are searched every night several times. No constable of the division had seen anyone with a bundle that morning.

The coroner announced that the body had not been identified, that the medical examination had not yet been completed, and that as Dr. Clarke was engaged at Bow-street to-day and could not attend, the inquest would be adjourned till ten o'clock next Tuesday morning.

THE CONCLUSIONS OF THE DOCTORS.

The cursory medical examination which has been made shows that the deceased had been a well-built woman, 5ft. 3in. in height, and between thirty and forty years of age. The measurement across the extended arms was 5ft. 4in,, and round the chest 31¾ in. The body was absolutely unclothed, but a portion of a linen under garment, much stained, had been thrown upon it. There were no marks to lead to identification, except a singular partially-healed semicircular wound, with a flap of skin adhering, on the index finger of the right hand. This wound might have been caused by a bite, or by a nail. The head had been removed, together with the legs from the hips, but the arms were intact. The latter were not developed muscularly, and the hands, long and slender, with albert-shaped nails, showed no signs of recent hard work. No ring-marks were detected, and nothing was noted which would indicate the woman's position in life or her calling, although an opinion was expressed that she might have been a factory hand or a rope-worker. The abdominal injuries were an imitation of what have been recorded in previous Whitechapel murders, but scarcely so fiendish in their character. The medical opinion was that death had taken place four or five days ago, and it is understood that the doctors also arrived at the conclusion that the dissecting-knife had been used by a left-handed person, who possessed considerable anatomical knowledge as well as physical strength. This peculiarity has been commented upon in former instances. No hacking was observable, and it was remarked that a saw had been employed as well as a knife. Until the post mortem examination is complete it is impossible to say in what manner the woman had come by her death, or whether she bad been subjected to an illegal operation.

IS THE CRIMINAL THE CHELSEA MISCREANT?

The police, until they are possessed of expert testimony on this and other points, refuse to commit themselves to any theory, but the resemblances to the facts disclosed in connection with the Rainham, Whitehall, and Battersea mysteries, were too remarkable to be overlooked by them. If the Chelsea dissector is still at work, and his motives were never made clear, he must, it is thought, have purposely removed his quarters to the East-end, or have conveyed the body which he wished to get rid of thither, with the intention of availing himself of the reputation of the undiscovered murderer, and to prevent a search being made for him in other parts of London. He may have taken this step, when he found that it was impossible, decomposition having set in, safely to dispose of the remains in any other way, but nevertheless he ran great risks of detection, for Whitechapel, owing to the dock strike, has latterly been full of police by day and by night. One circumstance which is favourable to the detectives is that if the man came from the West-end to the East he must have had a cart or a cab, as he could not have carried a bulky package in the dead of night without being noticed.

TWO EAST-END STORIES.

Among the stories current was one to the effect that a man carrying a sack was seen about eight o’clock on Monday evening a few yards from the spot where the body was found. It is stated that this person, apparently on observing a policeman some distance ahead, concealed himself in a gloomy corner of Christian-street, and that after the officer had passed on he reappeared but was then lost sight of, not, however, before his movements had aroused the suspicions of a labourer.

Last week a letter was found at the rear of the East London Hospital announcing the intention of the writer to perpetrate another murder immediately. The document was handed to the police; but no importance was attached to it in view of the number of such productions which have found their way into the hands of the authorities. Last night another letter was found in Whitechapel containing the following words:- “I told you last week I would do another murder.” Inquiries are being made to test the similarity of the writing.

SEARCHING THE THAMES CATTLE-BOATS.

On receiving intimation of the discovery a number of officers of the Thames Police, under Detective-inspector Regan, boarded vessels in the docks and at the mouth of the Thames, paying special attention to cattle-boats. The search occupied nearly the whole of the day, but was absolutely fruitless, the captain of each vessel being able to account for the movements of his crew during the early morning. The inquest is proceeding this morning at the Vestry Hall, Cable-street.

IS IT A HOAX BY A MEDICAL STUDENT?

The most experienced of the detectives who have been engaged in connection with the Whitechapel murders do not believe that Jack the Ripper has anything to do with the ghastly find of yesterday morning. They are of opinion that the body has been a “subject” in some dissecting-room, and that it was placed where it was discovered by some medical students who had obtained possession of it. A correspondent who advances this theory says: The police, it is believed, have this morning obtained an important clue in support of it. On the information being communicated to Superintendent Arnold he immediately left Whitechapel for Scotland-yard.

Exeter Flying Post - Wednesday 11 September 1889

THE LATEST WHITECHAPEL MYSTERY.

An important conference in connection with the latest murder in the East-end was held at the Whitechapel police station last evening. Dr.Phillips, divisional surgeon, who has been entrusted with the *post-mortem* and other investigations connected with most of the East End murders, was at Bournemouth for a holiday, and was telegraphed for. He arrived in London last evening and at once proceeded to Leman-street Station, where he was joined by Chief-Constable Colonel Monsell, Mr. Arnold, several officers from Scotland-yard, and Commissioner Munro. The strictest privacy was preserved regarding the deliberation, which lasted upwards of two hours. Mr. Munro and Dr. Phillips both refused to state what steps had been resolved upon by the authorities.

STATEMENT BY THE VIGILANCE CHAIRMAN.

Mr. Albert Backert, chairman of the Whitechapel Vigilance Committee writes as follows:- "As chairman of the last formed Whitechapel Vigilance Committee I have been questioned by a large number of people about to-day's discovery. From the time our committee was formed my colleagues and myself have done all in our power to discover the Whitechapel murderer. Night after night I have been out watching and making enquiries, but when the dock labourer's strike commenced the interest in the murders seemed to cool down, and thus several of my supporters relaxed the energy they had hitherto displayed. From enquiries, I am confident that the murderer is a Whitechapel person, or, at any rate, he is well acquainted with the back streets. It is a curious fact that in all places where these murders have occurred the houses are such that any person can enter by pulling a string, which lifts the latch. My opinion is that the murderer knows this, and the moment he has committed a murder he enters one of the houses. I firmly believe that if the police had searched the houses in the vicinity the moment the murder was discovered, the murderer would have been captured."

Cambridge Daily News - Wednesday 11 September 1889

A WHITECHAPEL MYSTERY.

Soon after the discovery of the ghastly bundle the police authorities drew a cordon of men around the neighbourhood. Inquiries in the vicinity did not result in anybody being discovered who had seen a person carrying a suspicious parcel, and persons living in some cottages in a court just opposite to the railway arch say they heard nothing at all unusual. That a person would hazard to walk far with suck a bulky and suspicious load seems incredible, and the police from this rather incline to believe that a murder has been committed in a house in the neighbourhood within the last three or four days, and that the murderer is disposing of the body piecemeal.

The people around the scene of the murder complain, with angry vehemence, of the infrequency of the police patrol. It is the rarest thing in the world they say to see a policeman round about these arches or the side streets contiguous.

So far as could bo elicited on Tuesday, the police are not very confident as to whether or not this latest horror should be ascribed to the same fiendish individual as the others that have horrified the community. The doctors, from their investigations, concluded that the cuts had been inflicted in a left-handed manner; that is to say, the cut in the throat was evidently commenced on the left side and carried to the right with a clean sweep. The same peculiarity was observed in the other wounds, and in separating the legs more flesh had been cut from the trunk on the left side than on the other. In more than one of the previous crimes this peculiarity had been observed and commented upon. The cut severing the head from the body was skilfully done, there being no hacking or clumsy dissection noticeable. Furthermore, a saw had been used to sever the bones in such a way as to leave no doubt that the person responsible for the dismemberment possessed good knowledge of anatomy. There were signs about the hands which would indicate that the woman had been used to hard work, and so far as could be seen there had been no attempt to obliterate a mark on one of the fingers, apparently caused by a ring. It is believed from certain indications that the deceased had never been a mother, but she might have been pregnant. The body was well-nourished and cared for. In consequence of the similarity of the mode of dismemberment pursued in this case and those of the recent Battersea and Rainham mysteries the officers engaged in those cases were consulted, and their general opinion is that the resemblance in the cases are so remarkable as to give grounds for the belief that the present crime is one with a different origin to the previous Whitechapel atrocities.

A conference, to which it believed considerable importance is attached, took place on Tuesday evening at Leman-street Police Station in connection with the Whitechapel murders. When Dr. Phillips was telegraphed for to Bournemouth on Tuesday morning, he replied that he would return to town at once, but to adjourn the *post-mortem* in the meantime. He arrived in London about 5 p.m. on Tuesday, and after making some preliminary investigations, attended at Leman-street Police Station soon after six o'clock. He was closeted with the Chief Constable, Colonel Monsell, Mr. Arnold, and the officers from Scotland-yard. At 7 p.m, Mr. Monro, the Chief Commissioner, arrived at the station in his private carriage, and joined in the deliberations, which continued until nearly half-past eight o'clock.

All the documents and reports concerning the discovery were examined carefully and discussed before Mr. Monro left Whitechapel. In answer to a representative of the press, the Chief Commissioner said he did not wish to make any statement regarding the proceedings. Dr. Phillips, in conversation with the representative of the Press Association, said as he had only just returned to town he did not wish to communicate to the press that which had been previously refused by his colleagues. He explained that being bound to secrecy he could express no opinion. Questioned as to whether he thought the murder was another of the series of crimes attributed Jack the Ripper, or whether it should rather be connected with the tragedies known as the Thames and Whitehall mysteries, he said he thought the reports published might be taken as fairly accurate. The police at Arbour-square Station have detained a sea-faring man on suspicion, but no importance is attached to his arrest. An incident came to light on Tuesday night which may be regarded as one of the curious circumstances in connection with the recent murder in this locality. Last week a letter was found at the rear of the East London Hospital announcing the intention of the writer to perpetrate another murder immediately. The letter was handed to the police, but no importance was attached to it in view of the number of such documents which have found their way into the hands of the authorities. On Tuesday night another letter was found in Whitechapel containing the following words:- "I told you last week I would do another murder." Inquiries are being made to test the similarity the writing of the documents. The police last night said there was nothing new to report in the way of clue or arrest.

The excitement in the district when the murder became known was very great, and groups gathered as near the fatal arch as the police permitted, and there discussed the latest horror in all its phases. There was no diminution in the crowd as the day wore on, many from outlying districts visiting the spot to satisfy their morbid tastes. Pinchin-street and its immediate neighbourhood is essentially a poor district, but the people residing there are mostly hard-working folk. It is singularly free from the degraded class of women who infest the courts and alleys of Whitechapel. The place is wretchedly lighted, and the many little dark passages about render the place like a rabbit warren, and peculiarly easy for a criminal to slip away undetected. Up till a late hour on Tuesday evening no arrest had been made in connection with the murder, and the police are absolutely without a clue of any kind. A circumstantial story to the effect that a suspicious-looking man was seen on Monday night carrying a sack near where the body was found proved, on investigation, to be entirely valueless.

The following statement has been made by a resident in Cable-street: "I was just taking down my shutters at half-past five o'clock last Tuesday morning, when a scavenger ran up to me and said, 'There's another Jack the Ripper job in Pinchin-street.' I at once ran over, and found there a policeman. I looked through the hoarding and saw just inside a woman's trunk completely naked. It had no doubt been dragged along the ground, as the pavement appeared as if this had been done. I did not see any blood about, or any marks around the aperture in the hoarding. The legs were cut off. So far as I could see the trunk was not ripped up, but it was turning purple. A woman living in another street, almost immediately opposite the arch, said she was awake all night through illness, but she heard no sound until the police blew their whistles at five o'clock on Tuesday morning. She said the locality was extremely quiet and ill-lighted, and the women were afraid to go about, as the arches were haunted by bad characters."

South Wales Echo - Wednesday 11 September 1889

THE HORRIBLE DISCOVERY IN WHITECHAPEL.

Latest Details.

Absolutely no Clue.

Nothing new has transpired in reference to the murder and mutilation in Whitechapel, and no arrests have been made. The police have made most careful inquiries at every cab-yard to ascertain whether any large parcel was carried in the direction of Pinchin-street stand. They have also searched thoroughly all disused warehouses and vacant spaces for the missing portions of the body, but without result. The police have absolutely no clue.

THE NINTH VICTIM.

London in general, and Whitechapel in particular, were thrown into a feverish state of excitement yesterday morning by the news that "Jack the Ripper" had murdered and mutilated his ninth victim. But the murder and the mutilation were reported to be, and indeed proved to be, more horrible than in any one of the eight cases preceding. The quick and close review of the facts by the police department led to the conclusion late yesterday afternoon that the remains found did not represent "Jack the Ripper's" handiwork, and this may or may not be true. There is a very extraordinary feature, however, in this case which has been lacking in all the others. That it is extraordinary no one will doubt who reads the brief story of last Saturday night as detailed below. If the woman found in the archway was a victim of "Jack the Ripper," it is positively sure either that the murderer has been seen by many people, or that another man who knew of the murder and all the circumstances so long ago as last Saturday night is abroad, and can be found if the police are clever enough. On the other hand, last Saturday night's events indicate to some extent that the body found yesterday, be it that of a murdered woman or a body from a dissecting room, was in the hands of more than one man who knew all about it, because last Saturday night a man betrayed the whole affair. The circumstances are as follows, and will be verified (says the *New York Herald*) in every particular by affidavit should the police department desire.

AN EXTRAORDINARY STORY.

Last Sunday morning, at five minutes past one o'clock, a young man called at the *Herald* office and reported that there was another "Jack the Ripper" murder. He was sent up to the editorial rooms and interviewed by the night editor. He said that a mutilated body had been found in Backchurch-lane, in Whitechapel. He said that it had been found by a policeman at twenty minutes past eleven o'clock. The map of London was immediately studied by two reporters in order to locate Backchurch-lane, while the editor cross-questioned the man. He said it had been told to him by an acquaintance of his, a police inspector whom he had met in Whitechapel High-street. He said there was no doubt about it, and that he had hurried to the *Herald* office understanding that be would be rewarded lor the news. He said his name was John Cleary, and that he lived at 21, White Horse Yard, Drury-lane. He was asked to write down his name and address, and did so, the writing being preserved. His information was explicit and seemingly authentic, and two reporters were detailed to take the man with them, and go and get the story.

The two reporters went out, and one of them stopped on the landing of the stairway in going down, and asked the man some more questions. Under this examination he varied slightly, saying that the man who had told him was not a police inspector, but an ex-member of the police force. This statement has, perhaps, some significance to all who have been following the murders closely. He then went down to the street with the reporters. They called a hansom and told the man to get in with them but he first hesitated, and then refused. His excuse was that it was too far from his home. They urged him to go, but he was firm. One of them proposed to take him back upstairs, in order to have him near at hand if necessary but the necessity of immediate departure compelled him to start and leave the man to go his own way. He was assured that if the news proved authentic he would be handsomely rewarded, and he went away apparently contented with the arrangement.

The two reporters drove rapidly to Blackchurch-lane. and found it without difficulty. They made a thorough search of the neighbourhood. They went down as far as the archway where the body was found yesterday morning, but found all quiet and no trace of any murder. They met two police officers, one an inspector and the other a constable. They questioned both, and told them the report they had heard, and these two officers can verity the enquiry. They had heard nothing, however. The reporters again went over the ground, but found nothing. They then returned and reported. In fact, it is a certainty that on Sunday morning a murdered and mutilated body was reported as having been found in Backchurch-lane, and that exactly such a body was found there yesterday morning.

The matter was passed over as unimportant on Sunday and Monday. The moment that the body was found yesterday, however, the events of Sunday morning loomed up with a significance rather colossal, and a hunt began for John Cleary, of 21, White Horse-yard, Drury-lane. Mr John Cleary, however, was not known at No. 21, or anywhere else in White Horse-yard, Drury-lane. The house is a four-story one. The street floor is vacant, the first and second floors are occupied by families, and the top floor by a widow woman with two children. The widow woman was confident that no young man by the name of John Cleary either lived in the house or had ever lived there. The people in every house in White Horse-yard were questioned under circumstances which disposed them to tell all they knew, but nobody had ever heard the name of John Cleary, and everybody said that no man of that name could have lived there without their knowing it, which was quite true. It became evident, therefore, that the man had given a false address, and in all probability a false name, as such a precaution in the matter of residence would scarcely have been taken, and the precaution as to name neglected.

"Cleary's" description, however, had been carefully taken. He was a young man, apparently between 25 and 28 years of age. He was short, his height being about 5ft, 4in. He was of medium build, and weighed about 140lb. He was light-complexioned, had a small fair moustache and blue eyes. On his left cheek was an inflamed spot, which looked as if a boil had lately been there and was healing. He wore a dark coat and waistcoat. His shirt was not seen, the space at the throat being covered by a dirty white handkerchief tied about his neck. His trousers were dark velveteen, so soiled at the knees as to indicate that be blacked shoes. His hat was a round, black, stiff felt. He walked with a shuffle and spoke in the usual fashion of the developing citizens of Whitechapel, whom, in all respects, he resembled.

It is thus certain that there was an intention on the part of the party or parties who had the body in keeping to place it in Backchurch-lane on Saturday night, where it was found yesterday. If coincidences be of any value, it may be noted that this was the anniversary of the Hanbury-street murder. It is beyond doubt that “Cleary” got wind of the scheme, if he was not one of the principals. That the original intention was not carried out would indicate that he was an outsider acquainted with the project who hoped to profit by it. There seemed to be no reason to doubt that the body was not found by the police until yesterday morning, and that it was placed there a short time before seems reasonably sure. Nevertheless, “John Cleary,” whoever he may be, must know all about the mystery, and is certainly the most valuable man in the purview of the police at the present time.

A Different Method of Mutilation.

A reperusal of the circumstances of former atrocities of this nature only serves to confuse the reader’s mind as to the possible origin of this last crime. It differs from the Whitechapel series in the facts that the head and lower limbs were amputated, and in the other fact that the hands were left undisturbed; but it resembles them in the infliction of the deep longitudinal cut along the lower half of the trunk. It will be remembered that last year, while the Whitechapel miscreant was in the full living of unchecked crime, a horribly mutilated human body was discovered in the basement storey of the building on the Embankment once intended for a national opera house. Here, too, the head and legs were missing, as in the case of the unfortunate woman found yesterday morning, but in this case the incomplete mutilation of the trunk had been completed in a fashion absolutely similar to that which marked the bodies of the Whitechapel victims. Nearly a month previously the right arm of a woman had been found floating in the Thames near Grosvenor-road railway bridge, and several indications justified the belief that it formed part of the body found later on in the basement of the opera house. The case of the girl whose mutilated remains were enveloped in a fragment of under garment, marked in black ink in a clear and clerkly hand with the name "L. E. Fisher," equally fails to offer any analogy to the other cases, as Dr Bond, chief surgeon of the Metropolitan Police, declared death to have resulted from an operation intended to procure abortion; a motive which could not have determined any of the Whitechapel series, and certainly did not exist in the present instance, as the medical testimony declares this last victim never to have been pregnant.

A Social Reproach.

The *Times* of to-day says:- "Unless this murder be the work of the Whitechapel murderer, and this is at least very much open to doubt, it may have been committed almost anywhere. It is not perhaps easy to determine which theory is the more disquieting. The impunity of the Whitechapel murderer is not only a source of real suffering to thousands of women far beyond the district in which he works and the class upon which he preys, but it is also of evil influence upon debased natures every- where, and may even become a useful screen for other criminals. On the other hand, it was, no doubt, a consolation for some people to think that his brutality worked only in a certain well-defined sphere, and that he is the only specimen of his class. But, in whichever way we take the matter, it cannot be denied that the list of conspicuous and unpunished crimes is already so long as to constitute a social reproach and disgrace, no matter how we may please to distribute the blame."

THESE INHUMAN MONSTERS.
What is to be Done?

One of the most repulsive features of these deeds of darkness, whether of the description attributed to "Jack the Ripper" or of that more scientific variety in which anatomical knowledge and dissecting expertness have been repeatedly displayed, is the deadly deliberateness with which their perpetrators go about them. These inhuman monsters (says the *Daily Telegraph*) lay their plans with faultless accuracy. They acquire exhaustive topographical acquaintance with the neighbourhood of the spot selected by them as the scene of their "coup"; they inform themselves to a nicety as to the habits of its population, the minutest details of its police organisation, the exact minute of each hour at which such and such a constable will pass through a certain street or turn a certain corner. Having "combined their information," made all its several items fit one another accurately, so as to make up a flawless programme of action, and provided against every conceivable contingency that could interfere with the execution of their project, or involve them in the slightest personal risk, they proceed to carry out their arrangements with a punctuality and precision that could not fail to crown any well devised and sagaciously ordered enterprise with success. The scoundrel who, between five a.m. and twenty minutes past that hour, deposited a woman's body under one of the Pinchin-street arches must have been familiar with every nock and corner, every twist and turn, of the labyrinthine complex of sordid streets, courts, and blind alleys surrounding the spot upon which he had resolved to rid himself of his gruesome burthen. He knew how to reach that locality unobserved, and how to get away from it unhindered. He knew exactly how much time he could dispose of for his operations between the recurrent perambulations of Pinchin-street by P.C Pannell. Everything came off exactly as he bad foreseen it would; no accident interposed between him and the perfect fruition of his scheme of action. What is to be done to prevent such cold-blooded, careful, intelligent malefactors as this, from indulging their criminal proclivities to the top of their bent, and with infallible impunity? Not only the authorities at the Home Office and Scotland Yard, but every right minded man and woman in the three kingdoms, have been asking this question in vain for many a month past. We all feel that something must be done; but what that something is to be none of us can tell. Meanwhile, it is little less than a national humiliation that a few ingenious miscreants should have succeeded, throughout two consecutive years, in baffling the entire police-force and detective capacity, professional and amateur, of this vast metropolis.

Difficulty of Identification.

The body of the deceased was removed to the St. George's Mortuary, and a large crowd gathered there directly, remaining throughout the whole day. Many "unfortunates" called to see the trunk, but none could identify it. In fact, there are no marks whatsoever on the remains which would enable anyone to conclusively identify the body, and, unless some other portions are discovered, it is quite possible that the matter will for ever remain a mystery, both as to who the woman was and who the murderers were. The police have no present knowledge of anyone corresponding with the deceased.

Excitement in the District.

The excitement in the district when the murder became known was very great, and groups gathered as near the fatal arch as the police permitted, and there discussed the latest horror in all its phases. There was no diminution in the crowd as the day wore on, many from outlying districts visiting the spot to satisfy their morbid tastes. At seven o'clock to-night there were no persons under arrest. The police are of opinion, though the deceased had been dead at least two days, that she was not murdered in the Whitechapel district, but in some more outlying suburb.

It is noteworthy that the police force in the district is at present much beyond its normal strength. The extra men who have been stationed in the district for some months past had not been withdrawn, but, on the contrary, their numbers had been reinforced in consequence of the dock strike. About that time the trunk was deposited under the arch some hundreds of constables were on their way from all parts of the metropolis through the neighbourhood en route to Leman-street police-station, where they are assembled to relieve the men who have done duty throughout the night.

× INDICATES WHERE THE BODY WAS FOUND.

DISCOVERY OF HUMAN REMAINS.

Scotch newspapers of August 31 give the following account of a discovery of human remains in Edinburgh:- “While one of the cleaners of the Union Canal, named Thomas Clark, was engaged in taking refuse from the canal near Fountain-bridge, he was horrified on bringing to the surface the left leg of a human being. The leg was not very much decomposed, and appeared to have been sawn off below the knee. It is supposed that a murder has been committed. Search is being instituted for more remains. The spot at which the limb was found is beside the city slaughterhouse.” It is suggested that inquiry should be made to ascertain whether the limb found in Edinburgh is a portion of the body found yesterday.

Western Daily Press - Thursday 12 September 1889

THE WHITECHAPEL MURDER.

LONDON, Wednesday Night. Although the police authorities have made most active investigations, nothing was gleaned by them to-day to elucidate the Pinchin Street mystery. Dr. Phillips and his assistants were occupied during the early part of the day in carefully examining the remains and preparing an exhaustive medical report upon the affair. They decline, however, to state anything concerning the case until the resumed inquest.

Up to the present the search for the missing portions of the body has not resulted in obtaining even a clue to work upon. Without the discovery of the head identification is rendered extremely difficult, and there are no distinctive marks or peculiarities upon the trunk. In previous cases of this sort in Whitechapel, the clothing has generally afforded a clue to identity, but the police are not similarly aided in the present instance.

To-day Superintendent Arnold and Inspector Reid were informed of some chalk writing on a wall at the corner of Frederick Street, a dark passage in the immediate proximity to the scene of the discovery. A name was introduced, with five or six other words written on the wall. The police do not, however, consider it a matter of much importance.

Several persons applied to police for permission to view the remains, but only those who could give reasonable cause were allowed to do so.

It is believed that the police have obtained a clue which will concentrate their investigations on an important shipping centre in the East End.

THE INQUEST.

Yesterday the inquest on the remains of the murdered woman was opened by the coroner, Mr Wynne Baxter, at St. George's Vestry Hall, Cable Street. Inspector Moore and Inspector Reid watched the inquiry on behalf of the police.

William Pennett, police constable 239 H, deposed: On Monday night I went on duty at ten o'clock.

Did anything attract your attention as unusual? - No, sir.

Had you a regular beat? - Yes, sir. I had to go through Pinchin Street at frequent intervals. The ground had took me half-an hour to cover. I always came from Christian Street into Back Church Lane. Sometimes I turned into Frederick Street, under the railway arches, and came back again into Pinchin Street. I usually returned then to the starting point in Pinchin Street.

At what time was it that you made this discovery? - About half-past five.

Which way did you come? - From the direction Christian Street into Back Church Lane.

What attracted your attention? - l was on the northern side of the road. I went across towards the railway arch.

You had no reason for doing it? - Just to look at the arch, sir. Before I got to the arch I saw the body there.

Perhaps that was the reason for going? - Well, I often look there, not always.

What did you see? - l saw a bundle like some of the Jews throw away sometimes. The arch belongs to the vestry, and leads to a piece of waste ground between two lines of railway. Two of the arches are closed in with a fencing about 10 or 12 feet high. The arch in which I found the body contains only the uprights and crossbars of the fencing, the planks having been taken away. There are road stones piled in various places. There is a cart entrance to this enclosed ground by a gate in Back Church Lane.

What was the position of the bundle? - lt was four and half to five yards in the archway, measured from the pavement.

Was it near wall of the arch? - Yes, sir; on the western side.

On going up to it, what did you find? - I found that it was not a bundle, but the remains a human body.

Was it covered? - There were two or three pieces of rag on it. What they were I could not say at the time. Otherwise, it was naked.

I suppose you noticed at once that the whole body was not there? - l noticed that the head had been taken from the body, and two legs were missing. The trunk was lying east and west, with the shoulders towards the west.

Was it a dusty place? - Yes, sir.

Did you notice any marks of wheels? - No, sir.

Or footprints? - No; the dust would not leave a good impression.

Were there any drops of blood about? - None.

What did you do? - I did not know whether to blow my whistle or not, as, being so early in the morning, it would have only caused a large crowd to assemble. I waited a minute or two beside the lifeless body, and a man came along with a broom. I said him, “You might go and fetch my mate at the corner.” He said, “What’s on, governor;” I said, “Tell him I’ve got a job. Make haste.”

Did he go? - He then went up Back Church Lane towards the adjoining beat, where my mate was. I next saw two constables running towards me. No. 205 H, the acting sergeant, was first to arrive, and 115 followed. I said, “You had better go and see the inspector, as there is a dead body here.” No. 205 ran off to the station, and 115 remained with me, and before long I saw Inspector Pinhorn.

Did anyone pass up to that time? - No, sir; I saw no one.

Did you then make a search? - Yes. We found two men asleep in the last arch, who had the appearance of sailors. They were a short distance apart. In the middle arch there was a shoeblack lying on the stones.

Were they all asleep? - The shoeblack was asleep; we had to wake him up.

And the sailors? - The first one was asleep, but I am uncertain whether the other one was or not. He had a pipe in his mouth. They were taken to the station.

Did they make any statement to you? - No, sir.

Can you fix the time when you passed this place before? - Before five.

Any nearer than that? That might be five minutes past four, you know. - 1 know it was all that, because coming along the night before a working man asked me to call him when I passed through Pinchin Street.

You mean just before five? - Yes, sir.

Did you look in the arch then? - Yes.

Did you cross over? - No; I looked across the road. I did not cross right over.

Was it light at five? - Not exactly light; it was just before the break of day. I did not see anything in the arch. Had it been there I should have seen it. After I left Pinchin Street I went along Church Lane to Christian Street. I did not see anyone with a bundle. I did not see a costermonger's cart moving. I saw a barrow in Spitt Street. I saw no cart or vehicle about except in Christian Street, where there were some lying about. None came down Pinchin Street. Dr. Clarke arrived within half an hour of the discovery of the body. The remains were removed to the mortuary soon after six o'clock. I don't know whether the arches are often used for sleeping. It is the first time I have been on the beat.

In reply to a juror, the witness said the body looked as though it had been emptied out of a sack or something of the sort. There were no marks of sand or gravel on the trunk. There were no marks of a trail in the dust. The ground was not disturbed.

By Inspector Reid: There was a lot of stones and rubbish as well as dust in the archway, and there were no signs of a struggle having taken place.

A Juror: If you had seen a man carrying a bundle, would you have stopped him? - Certainly.

And any other constable would have done the same? - Yes.

Inspector Pinhorn deposed: Shortly after halfpast five o'clock I heard of the discovery, and went to the spot at once. I ordered a search, and assisted in it. We searched the arches and the piece of vacant ground. A crowd began to collect, and I had the street cleared. Statements were taken at the station from the men found in the arches. They stated that when they went to the arches there was nothing there, and they heard no sound. Two of the men went there at four o'clock, and one went at two o'clock.

The Coroner: Do you know whether these arches are used by casuals? - They would be if we did not prevent them. We prevent them as far as possible, and turn them out night after night.

Would a person who knew the neighbourhood well know there was a probability of sleepers being there? - That class of person would know it. The ground belongs to the Whitechapel District Board of Works, having been exchanged by the St. George's Vestry. It is used for stonebreaking.

Inspector Reid: The police have no right in there? - Oh, no. Still, extraordinary precautions have been taken for some time past. All isolated spots have been searched through the night.

Inspector Reid said he had interrogated the three men found under the arches. They had been drunk, and, having no money to pay for lodging, slept under the arches.

The Coroner: It is a curious circumstance that the whole of the ground is properly guarded except this one arch? - I don't know about properly guarded, for the palings put all round are of a very temporary character. Yesterday, in Back Church Lane, I had considerable difficulty in preventing the people trying to look through from pulling the railings down.

Without going into the evidence, did any constable notice anyone with a bundle that morning? - 1 have ascertained that none did.

A bundle of that nature would attract attention? - Yes.

Do you know whether costermongers are about with anything on them at that time in the morning? - Costermongers would not be passing in that direction. I see no reason for it. They would be passing towards Spitalfields Market.

They would not be coming from Spitalfields Market? - No. Costermongers are not the first to buy, like tradesmen. Their barrows do not leave the market till six o'clock.

I suppose a general search of the whole neighbourhood was made? - Yes; without anything being found bearing on the case.

Did these people say whether the body was there when they went? - Well, they did not see it.

Could they say it was not there? - Their condition did not enable them to go beyond that. (Laughter.) There is a lamp from 12 to 20 yards from the spot, but it is so situated that it throws a light on the archway but not a shadow. The body was found lying from 8ft. to 9ft. from the footway. The ground under the arch lies 15 inches lower than the footway. The position of the trunk was such as to indicate it had been carried in a sack, or closely bound up together. The arms were close to the body, and the hands beneath the abdomen. The chemise was cut jaggedly, and made to appear like rags. It was an old chemise, and had been worn some time.

I must have it accurately described. I don't know whether you will do it. What material was it made of? - Calico.

Was it well made? Hand-made or machine made? - Machine made. It was very old, such as the very poor class of women wear. There was no lace on it. There were large bloodstains it, though it was not saturated.

Was there blood on the body? - No, not much.

Had it been washed? - No, I should say not, from the somewhat dirty appearance.

I suppose there is no name on the chemise? - None. There are no marks at all, and nothing to identify it.

We shall have a full description, of course, from medical witnesses, to the state of the body, so that we need not go into that.

The Coroner said Dr. Clarke, who first saw the body could not attend that day, and Dr. Phillips was at present making a careful examination of the body. As the body had not been identified – perhaps not a hopeless task, though, a difficult one - it would be well to adjourn the inquiry.

The inquest was accordingly adjourned till ten o'clock on the 24th inst.

The people residing near the scene of the discovery complain, with angry vehemence, the infrequency of police patrol. It is the rarest thing in world, they say, to see a policeman round about those arches or the side streets contiguous. One man declared that a short time since a woman was screaming murder at the top of her voice for 20 minutes about four o'clock in the morning, and no policeman was attracted to the spot. It was nothing very serious, said the man, "only some joker beating his wife," but he thought it showed how unprotected those parts were about there. The uniformed and plain-clothed-police force have for a long time past been unusually strong - much more so probably than the inhabitants have themselves been aware of, and it is well known that the trouble between the Dock Companies and their labourers have added immensely to the work of the force, though there may have been no actual need for their services. “I have been nineteen hours on duty,” said one of the sergeants on Tuesday, bewailing the hard times they were getting between the strikes on the one hand and the unknown murderers other; “and of course,” he continued, “plenty of other men have done the same.”

On Tuesday night another letter was found in Whitechapel, containing the following words:- “l told you last week I would do another murder.”

It is a somewhat remarkable fact that one of the Whitechapel murders of last year took place on September 8. Consequently the present crime must have been perpetrated at a time only a few hours removed from the exact anniversary of a previous atrocity.

Dr. Forbes Winslow writes as follows:- “Between the murder of July and the latest atrocity, in consequence of a statement I made, I have been inundated by innumerable communications. I received intimation that on August 30th, under many of the arches in Whitechapel the following was seen on walls: ‘Jack the Ripper is now going to commit another murder in this neighbourhood.’ I was on the point of informing the police of this, but was told that they must have seen it. I found that they did see it, and as fast as it was written they rubbed it out again, not even seeing or catching the writer. It would be interesting to know whether such a warning is always treated as a joke? What I have heard of the latest crime in every way agrees with the most important evidence in my possession as to the way of tracing and capturing the individual. I believe that were the proper steps taken to carry out a carefully thought-over plan, but of which as a private individual I do not care to risk the responsibility or the expense, that he could be found within a week, and I do not hesitate to so positively express this assertion."

Pall Mall Gazette - Thursday 12 September 1889

THE WHITECHAPEL MYSTERY.
STILL NO CLUE.

Notwithstanding the active exertions of the police authorities, practically nothing was gleaned by them yesterday tending to elucidate the mystery surrounding the death of the woman whose mutilated remains were discovered on Tuesday morning in Pinchin-street, Whitechapel. No arrests have been made. The streets and alleys of the district fairly bristle with policemen, some in uniform, and others in plain clothes.

WHAT WAS DONE YESTERDAY.

Dr. Phillips and his assistants were busily occupied for six hours yesterday in carefully examining the remains and preparing an exhaustive medical report upon the case. The trunk will be preserved in spirits, and will not be buried for the present. Mr. Monro, Chief Commissioner of Police, Colonel Monsoll, Assistant-Commissioner, and Superintendent Arnold were in consultation nearly an hour yesterday. Dr. Phillips, it is understood, verbally informed Mr. Monro of the result of the examination, and he will make a formal report, which will probably be in the Chief Commissioner's hands this morning. The police have carried out a careful examination of all places where they might possibly find the missing portion of the body, or the locality where the murder was perpetrated. Up to the present, however, the detectives have learned nothing to reward their efforts.

THE DIFFICULTIES IN THE WAY OF IDENTIFICATION.

Of course, without the head, identification is a matter of the utmost difficulty, as the body does not appear to have any distinguishing marks or peculiarities. Neither is much assistance afforded in this direction by the torn and blood-stained under-garment which partially enveloped the trunk. In most of the previous East-end murders the clothing has aided in the identification, and it will be recollected that the marking upon some of the underclothing found with the Battersea remains eventually enabled the police to trace the movements of the murdered woman up to within a comparatively short time previous to her death. The railway arch under which Tuesday's discovery was made has now been completely boarded up.

EXCITEMENT IN THE DISTRICT.

Among the women and girls of the district in which the remains were found, many of whom work till late in the night, there is a dread to leave the friendly shelter of their homes and on Tuesday night, though the crowd in the locality of the discovery was very large during the early part of the evening, scarcely any one ventured near the spot after nightfall, the police being left the solitary guardians of the place.

HOW THE GRUESOME PARCEL MIGHT BE CARRIED UNNOTICED.

The whole neighbourhood is essentially the home of the sweater. Whole streets and alleys are occupied by men who employ girls and lads in the tailoring and other trades. They work in dingy, stuffy rooms, in dilapidated buildings. Not only are they employed here during the day, but night after night they work on until midnight. Then, with parcels containing large quantities of materials, they return to their homes. The material they so convey is usually worked at home by their parents or others. This fact alone would account for the ease with which a person could convey a large parcel through even a crowded thoroughfare in this locality at almost any hour during the night. In the opinion of the police, the trunk found was so conveyed by a person who must have had a thoroughly intimate acquaintance, not only with the geography of the locality, but with the habits and customs of the people.

Nottingham Evening Post - Thursday 12 September 1889

WHITECHAPEL MYSTERY.

There has been no fresh information gained this morning regarding the mysterious discovery in Pinchin-street, though every effort is being put forward by the police and others to gain a clue to the matter. As the result of the post-mortem examination made last evening a small quantity of fluid was found in the stomach, leading to the belief that the woman was drugged or poisoned. An analysis of the contents of the abdomen will be made.

IS IT A HOAX?

The most experienced of the detectives who have been engaged in connection with the Whitechapel murders do not believe that Jack the Ripper has anything to do with the ghastly find. They are of opinion that the body has been a "subject" in some dissecting-room, and that it was placed where it was discovered by some medical students who had obtained possession of it. A correspondent who advances this theory says: The police, it is believed, have obtained an important clue in support it. On the information being communicated to Superintendent Arnold he immediately left Whitechapel for Scotland-yard.

STILL ANOTHER THEORY.

It has been suggested that the person who deposited the body in the archway had brought it to the locality along the railway line which runs above the arches. Having arrived at the spot, he watched the policeman out of sight, then having fixed a rope to one of the trucks standing on the arch, slid down the rope with the bundle in his arm or attached to him in some way. Having carefully deposited the body, all he had to do was to climb up this rope again, and from behind the parapet of the arch, watch for the discovery, and laugh in his sleeve at the fruitless search for himself.

Morning Post - Friday 13 September 1889

THE EAST-END MURDER.

Inquiries made late last night at the Leman-street Police-station, where the officers of the H Division, under Superintendent Arnold, have all along had the case in hand, produced nothing beyond the statement that the minute and exhaustive investigation which has been going on for the last two days and a half has hitherto failed to produce the slightest information likely to lead either to the identification of the poor creature whose headless trunk was found in the Pinchin-street archway, or to the faintest clue to the criminal. Although, of course, the Home Office has been fully apprised of everything that has come to the ears of the Chief Commissioner since the body was found, no reward has yet been offered for the arrest of the criminal, and it is not at present deemed likely that such a course will be resorted to. No persons are in custody in connection with the murder.

South Wales Daily News - Friday 13 September 1889

THE WHITECHAPEL OUTRAGE.
POST-MORTEM EXAMINATION.
THE POLICE NONPLUSSED.

As the result of the fullest investigation, the police are still without a clue to the identity of the dead woman, whose mutilated body was discovered early on Tuesday morning lying in a railway arch off Pinchin-street, St George's-in-the-East. Neither is there any indication, or suspicion, pointing to the author of what is now believed to have been an atrocious crime. The medical examination has made it quite clear that the cause of death was syncope, caused by hemorrhage, but there is no evidence to prove in what manner the loss of blood was produced; still little doubt is entertained that it followed upon some act of violence, perhaps the fracture of the skull, or, more probably; the cutting of the throat. It is understood that there is no reason to support the theory that the woman had been subjected to an unlawful operation, from the consequences of which she died. Her condition negatives any such supposition. There is no confirmation of the assertion that the injuries were inflicted by a left-handed man; on the contrary, the cutting seems to have been done with the right. The one fact left undisputed is that the deceased met with her death in no ordinary way, and if she was murdered, the deed must have been accomplished by some person with an insufficient motive. For taking all the appearances together, it is supposed that the victim was of a low stamp, belonging probably to the same class as the woman whose remains were thrown into the Thames at Chelsea or concealed in Battersea Park. The resemblances between the Pinchin-street and Chelsea cases are positively startling, and there is warrant for believing that the dissecting-knife had been employed by the same hand in both instances.

THE POST-MORTEM EXAMINATION.

Dr Phillips, divisional surgeon of police; Dr Hibbert, professor of anatomy at Westminster Hospital; and other medical men, have made a careful post-mortem examination of the trunk. Their opinion is that the woman had not been dead more than from three to four days when her trunk was discovered. On opening the stomach there was found a small quantity of liquid, which, from its appearance, gave no impression that the unfortunate woman had been stupefied by some drug, or that she had even met her end by poison. For this reason it is not unlikely that Dr Stevenson, the toxicological expert, will be called upon to make an analysis of the viscera and contents of the stomach, which have been carefully preserved. That such an analysis will take place is considered certain, inasmuch as no absolute disease sufficient to account for death was discovered, nor were there any wounds, beyond, of course, the amputation of the head and limbs, on the body. There was, it is stated, a small amount of internal inflammation, the cause of which could not be ascertained. Upon a careful examination of the arms, four distinct bruises were noticeable, and these, in the opinion of the medical experts, were occasioned by the woman's struggles with her murderer. The body was well nourished, and the age is now supposed to be about 25, Dr Clarke and Dr Phillips, after an examination of the hands, having, it is stated, come to that conclusion. The trunk now lies in methylated spirits. The trunk weighs about 70lb.

Pall Mall Gazette - Saturday 14 September 1889

THE WHITECHAPEL MYSTERY.

At present no information has been obtained as to the identity of the woman whose body was found mutilated and dismembered in Pinchin-street; or has any fresh discovery been made tending to throw any light either on the crime or the personality of the murderer. The authorities have published and circulated the following description of the remains of the woman, with a view, if possible, of getting them identified: Aged about thirty-five years: height 5 ft. 3 in.; hair dark brown; skin fair; hands soft and shapely, nails well kept; small circular hardening, but no corn, on right little finger; arms small but well shaped; body plump and well formed, with full breasts. No marks of rings on fingers, and no evidence of maternity. The East-end has assumed its normal aspect, and the recent discovery in St. George's, like its predecessors, or perhaps a little more speedily, has lapsed into a thing of the past. The authorities are absolutely without a clue, and no one is detained on suspicion.

Daily Gazette for Middlesbrough - Saturday 14 September 1889

THE LONDON HORRORS. UNFOUNDED REPORT OF ANOTHER MURDER.

It was rumoured in London early this morning that another murder had been committed in the East End. On enquiry, however, the Press Association learns that the report is entirely unfounded.

THE DISCOVERY IN WHITECHAPEL. STILL NO CLUE.

It is now considered probable that more than one person knew of the crime from a significant circumstance. Mr Packer, whose declaration that he could identify the author of the Berner-street murder excited some amount of interest, has been attacked and injured. Shortly after the commission of the murder preceding the Pinchin-street discovery Packer again expressed an opinion that the criminal did not live "very far from Batty-street," which is within three minutes' walk of the railway arch. Not long after that Packer averred that while he was standing near his doorstep two men rushed upon him and knocked him down, with the remark, "Know where 'Jack the Ripper' lives, do you?" The unfortunate man was, as a result, admitted to the London Hospital, where he was detained for three weeks.

Nothing new has transpired in connection with the Pinchin-street mystery. The detectives have nothing whatever to work upon.

Bury Free Press - Saturday 14 September 1889

PINCHIN STREET

ANOTHER WHITECHAPEL ATROCITY.

“Whitechapel again!” has become the telegraphic code signal of the metropolitan police, and now only needs to be sounded to bring to bear on Whitechapel the scrutiny of the whole force. Yet in spite of the most elaborate system, the most careful organization, and the most rigorous surveillance, another of those terrible crimes which have shocked the whole country has been coolly perpetrated, almost within a stone’s throw of the city boundary. The scene of the latest Whitechapel murder is within five minutes’ walk of the Tower, and quite close to Leeman-street police station. The body was found under one the arches of the East London Railway, which runs from Fenchurch-street to the Docks. Pinchin-street is a short narrow street with the railway arches on one side, and a few cottages on the other. It leads out of

Backchurch-lane, which is reached either from Whitechapel High-street or from Cable-street, a narrow but busy thoroughfare, leading east from the Minories. The whole locality is full of wretched slums, and just the place it might be assumed a murderer would select for his horrible work.

Manchester Courier and Lancashire General Advertiser - Saturday 14 September 1889

THE WHITECHAPEL OUTRAGE.

Nothing has transpired to throw any further light upon the latest Whitechapel mystery. It is believed that the woman must have been murdered at the house or apartments of the murderer, as if she had been killed in her own rooms her absence would have been noticed. The police would be glad of any information respecting women having gone to the houses of single men under suspicious circumstances.

The following amended description was circulated by the police at the close of the post-mortem:- "Age of deceased about 33, height 5ft. 3 in., hair dark brown, skin fair, hands soft and shapely, nails well kept; a small circular hardening but no corn on right little finger, arms small but well shaped, body plump and well formed, with full bust; no marks of rings on fingers, no evidence of maternity.

The detectives are still searching for the man named Leary or Cleary, who on Sunday last went to a newspaper office and reported that a woman had been murdered in Back Church-lane, Whitechapel. A full description of this man has been obtained, and it is believed that before many hours his whereabouts will be known.

Wishing to find out whether there is anything in the theory which has been suggested, and which has become somewhat popular in the East-end, that the trunk of the woman found in Pinchin-street, last Tuesday morning has come from some dissecting room, a correspondent of the *Pall Mall Gazette* called at the London Hospital and had a chat with one of the resident surgeons.

"I am not at all surprised," said the doctor, smiling, "that many people think this affair a hoax on the part of medical students. It is, of course, within the range of possibility that students may get possession of a body; but as to the theory that this particular trunk has been taken from some dissecting room, it is really, in my opinion, absurd. It is the most unlikely thing in the world that a trunk should be in a state in which I understand this one to be in, after being in the dissecting room. It is against dissecting room rules that it should be as it is."

"Will you kindly explain how?"

"Well, you see, there are standing rules for dissecting bodies. The corpse is dissected in a thoroughly systematic fashion. It is left almost entirely to the students. The body is laid out on the dissecting table, and each student takes a certain part. By the time a body is dissected it is, as you may imagine, quite unrecognisable."

“Is it a fact, as you have seen alleged, that it is a common thing for students to possess themselves of portions of bodies after dissection?”

“Oh, yes. They often take away a foot or a hand, but it is not very likely that the would cart home a head or a leg.”

“What, may I ask, is done with the remains after dissection?”

“The different portions are collected and the whole buried together.”

“May I inquire where you get your dissecting room subjects from here?”

“We get them generally from the workhouse, as at Cambridge, where the workhouse authorities have a sort of stock supply.”

“Could students obtain a body from the workhouse on their own account?”

“Well, that I can’t say. It might be possible for them to do so. I may observe so long as I remember that even if this trunk affair is a hoax by medical students, none of our young men have anything to do with it, because they are all away just now. This is vacation time, and the dissecting room is not open.”

“From what you have heard about this trunk, do you think that great surgical skill must have been possessed by the person or persons who dismembered it?”

“Of course I have not seen the remains, and I can only go by what I have read and heard; but let me say that it is ridiculous to talk about surgical skill in the way that people are doing in connection with the Whitechapel horrors. Any butcher could do what has been done in any of the cases, this trunk case included. One does not necessarily require to be a doctor or a medical student to be able to dismember a body. I think there has been rather too much made of this point in connection with the murders."

Penny Illustrated Paper - Saturday 14 September 1889

ANOTHER WHITECHAPEL MURDER: DISCOVERY OF THE VICTIM IN THE RAILWAY ARCH.

Gloucester Citizen - Monday 16 September 1889

THE WHITECHAPEL TRAGEDY.

At present no information has been obtained as to the identity of the woman whose body was found mutilated and dismembered in Pinchin-street, nor has any fresh discovery been made tending to throw any light either on the crime or the personality of the murderer. The East end has assumed its normal aspect, and the recent discovery, like its predecessors, or perhaps a little more speedily, has lapsed into a thing of the past. The authorities are absolutely without a clue, and no one is detained on suspicion.

A remarkable story was current of an ordinarily well-dressed man, who lived in a house in the suburbs by himself, his wife having left him. At the time of the seventh murder in Whitechapel this man, having sold his furniture hurriedly, left the locality on the plea that he was about going abroad. Then it dawned upon one of his neighbours that the individual in question came home on the morning of one of the murders in such altered garb as to astonish those who had known him. His explanation - that he had so dressed as a practical joke - was accepted, while to account for some blood on his clothes he said he had been assaulted. The man is said to have been recently seen in London, and on the morning the horrible discovery was made in Pinchin-street it is now believed he was in that district. In answer to inquiries at the station at Leman-street the police stated that nothing was known there of the matter.

On Saturday night, at a quarter-past seven, there was found in the waters of the river Thames off Charing-cross railway bridge a woman's calico chemise, done up in some newspapers, which, on being examined, was found to have blood-stains, especially at the back, just below the neck, whilst the garment was partly torn in a straight line downwards. The police authorities are adopting extra measures for the better supervision of the Whitechapel district, and on Saturday night 100 extra policemen were drafted from other districts to Whitechapel for the purpose of being duty there for the next three months.

During the sermon at York Minster yesterday Canon Fleming preaching to a crowded congregation made special reference to the Whitechapel murders, which had baffled the intelligence of the whole police force. Referring to the scene of the murder he said many houses were not fit for pigs to live in. He was thankful to say that many noblemen, including the Duke of Westminster and the Duke of Bedford, were doing their utmost to abolish these dens of filth and vice, and to get the inhabitants to live sober, industrious lives, and thus improve their position, which he contended was due entirely to intemperance.

Lancashire Evening Post - Monday 16 September 1889

THE WHITECHAPEL MURDER.

The Press Association says the position of affairs in connection with the latest East End murder was a midnight practically unaltered. The result of the investigation of a parcel taken out of the river on

Saturday night is not such to connect the discovery with the recent murder, although it is regarded as sufficiently suspicious to warrant immediate attention. The garment was a woman's chemise in a filthy state, with some stains of blood, but the police do not believe it belongs to the victim of the Pinchin tragedy. There is still no clue to the identity of the murdered woman.

THE POLICE THEORY.

The question as to whether there is a secret murderous gang with headquarters in the East-end or some other part of London is now exercising the minds of the authorities at Scotland Yard, as the police are almost satisfied that the latest crime was known to more than one man. Inspector Tonbridge and Inspector Swanson are pursuing their investigations, but at present it is stated there is but the smallest possible clue. The issue, however, has been somewhat narrowed. If the murder was the work of one man, his abode, the police assert, must be close to Pinchin-street; if the deed was not committed in Whitechapel, then the trunk could not have been conveyed so great a distance unless the miscreant had a vehicle at his disposal, and the most exhaustive inquiries at cab-yards, of carmen, and at places where barrows are lent on hire, have produced an absolutely negative result. That more than one person knew of the crime is considered probable from a significant circumstance, thought little of at the time, in connection with Mr. Packer, whose declaration that he could identify the author of the Berner-street murder excited some amount of interest. Shortly after the commission of the murder preceding the Pinchln-street discovery, Packer again expressed an opinion that the criminal did not "live very far from Batty-street," which is within three minutes' walk of the railway arch. Not long after that Packer averred that while was standing near his doorstep two men rushed upon him and knocked him down, with the remark, "Know where Jack the Ripper lives, do you?" The unfortunate man was, as a result, admitted to the London Hospital, where he was detained for three weeks.

A PARALLEL TO THE LEARY INCIDENT

It seems the remarkable story told of the visit paid by the man Leary to the London office of the *New York Herald* is not without parallel in connection with the revolting crimes which in the past 18 months have occurred in the metropolis. The Leary incident has recalled the fact that a few nights before the horrible discovery of the dead body of a murdered woman in one of the recesses of the basement of the new offices intended as the headquarters of the metropolitan police on the Victoria Embankment, a man answering the same description entered the office of the *Morning Advertiser* and stated that the remains of a woman were to be found in that spot. The man asked a fee for the information, but before this was paid a reporter was despatched to the buildings to ascertain, with the aid of the police, whether there was any foundation for the story. Search was made in vain as in Back Church-lane the other day, but a day or two afterwards the mutilated body of a female was discovered in the precise spot which had been indicated by the mysterious informant.

Taunton Courier, and Western Advertiser - Wednesday 18 September 1889

THE EAST END MURDER

As the result of the fullest investigation, the police are still without a clue to the identity of the dead woman. Neither is there any indication, or suspicion, pointing to the author of what is now believed to have been an atrocious crime. The medical examination has made it quite clear that the cause of death was syncope, caused by haemorrhage, but there is no evidence to prove in what manner the blood loss was produced; still little doubt is entertained that it followed upon some act of violence perhaps the fracture of the skull, or, more probably, the cutting of the throat. It is understood that there is no reason to support the theory that the woman had been subjected to an unlawful operation, from the consequence of which she died. Her condition negatives any such supposition. There is no confirmation of the assertion that the injuries were afflicted by a left-handed man; on the contrary, the cutting seems to have been done with the right. The one fact is left undisputed. That the deceased met with her death in no ordinary way, and if she was murdered, the deed must have been accomplished by some person with an insufficient motive. For, taking all the appearances together, it is supposed that the victim was of a low stamp, belonging, probably, to the same class as the woman whose remains were thrown into the Thames at Chelsea or concealed in Battersea Park. The resemblances between the Pinchin-street and Chelsea cases are positively startling, and there is warrant for believing that the dissecting knife had been employed by the same hand in both instances.

Without entering into particulars, one point may be mentioned. In the most recent murder the injuries to the abdomen appear to have been commenced in exactly the same way as in the Chelsea case; but the operator seems to have abandoned his task half-way, and not made a cross-cut, or the parallel would have been complete. It is important to bear in mind that the use of the knife in this instance differs essentially from the manner in which the steel was employed upon the body of the Dorset-street victim last November. In discussing the various theories which arise, the Dorset-street case is always cited as having been the only Whitechapel murder which occurred in a room. It is held that the Pinchin-street and Chelsea murders, assuming them to have been such, must also have been perpetrated in some apartment, but there is this difference between them, Whereas the Dorset-street mutilations were of the most brutal kind, surpassing in ferociousness anything which the mind can conceive, and evidencing a perfect fury of passion on the part of the man, the Pinchin-street dismemberment was of the opposite character, testifying to nerve and self-command, as well as to skill. In the Chelsea case the same peculiarities were observed, and hence there is considered to be some ground for the deduction that the West-end dissector has transferred his operations to the East. Up to the present no adequate reason has been shown why Jackson, a poor, unfortunate woman, should have been way-laid and put cruelly to death by some man who had at his command special facilities for concealment; but, nevertheless, Jackson did meet her end in a mysterious manner, and some individual – still at large – put himself to infinite pains to distribute portions of her body in various parts of Chelsea, with the hope of destroying all traces of the crime which must have taken place.

To make detection less likely he removed the head. This same plan was carried into practice in Pinchin-street. The inference drawn is that in each instance the murdered woman had probably been seen in the company of the man who would on that account take care that no one should recognise the features of the deceased, lest a witness should be forthcoming to prove that she had entered a certain house, from which she had never emerged alive. That the latest victim did not belong to Whitechapel is considered to be likely from the absence of enquiries for missing women in the locality of the crime. The feeling in the district, generally, is that the remains were brought into the neighbourhood from some place at a distance. This transportation need not necessarily have been done at night; for, although the body was decomposing, the process of decay had not advanced very far, and it is conceded to be quite possible that death had even occurred within thirty-six hours of the discovery. The ghastly burden may, therefore, it is suggested, have been carried in a barrow, at dusk or in open daylight, from another part of the metropolis, and the moment might have been chosen for depositing the trunk in the place where it was found. If, however, the transference took place at night, there would be nothing unusual in the sight of a laden coster's barrow being wheeled along, and the circumstances would certainly not attract much attention; but it is pointed out that any man coming, say, from Chelseawould, unless he hazarded the venture, have to be quite sure of his plans in advance to enable him to make use of a remote place of concealment, and he must have fixed upon the arch as his destination – unless it should subsequently be shown that he had some shelter in St. George's in which to wait, such as a humble lodging would have afforded. It is a fact, however, that no statements have been volunteered tending to incriminate any person living in the vicinity of the crime.

One circumstance was a few days ago reported to the police, which, if capable of substantiation, would have proved that on Sunday the fact that a murder had been committed in Backchurch-lane, or thereabouts, was known to a man giving the name of "Joe Cleary," and supplying a false address in Drury-lane. The information which this man furnished was conveyed to the police, who satisfied themselves that it had no foundation, and it is now believed that the story originated with the man having seen or heard of a drunken woman who was taken away upon a stretcher from a place near to Cable-street on the night in question. In connection with the same matter it was pointed out to the police that some writing in chalk upon a fence in Frederick-street, Cable-street, partly obliterated, included Cleary's name, but not much importance was attached to this coincidence.

Meanwhile there is no testimony of any kind to clear up the mystery which surrounds the discovery. Whitechapel may have acquired the notoriety that deeds of horror may there be committed with impunity, but the police arrangements have in no way been relaxed, and short of stationing a constable at every doorpost, no better system of protection or of precaution can be devised than that which has been for some time arranged. The strike, moreover, has brought about a large augmentation of the local forces. All these points are matters of common knowledge, and for that reason it is imagined that the person desirous of concealing the body profited perhaps more by chance than by design. Possibly he may have been making his way to the river, when the deserted arch offered him the opportunity for which he was in search. Why the man should have deliberately selected the arch, when he must have know that discovery in the course of a few hours, or even minutes, was inevitable, cannot be otherwise explained, except on the supposition, which in some quarters has been advanced, that the veritable Whitechapel murderer is again active, with the sole object of surpassing in daring his previous terrible exploits. But the question is anxiously asked – where can he live, where does he hide his surgical knives and saws, where can he take his victims without attracting suspicion, and what garb does he assume? A disguise of some sort must have been necessary if the body were wheeled upon a barrow by any man not a coster. The old slaughterman theory has been revived; but one of that trade living in a single room would be as much open to observation as anyone else, if he attempted the practice of his calling at home, and it is obvious that he could not use his employer's premises for murdering and dissecting women. If the miscreant, or miscreants, are not of this class, then it is admitted that the must have some connection with professions and avocations which would enable them to acquire the necessary skill, and to avoid the idle curiosity of their neighbours. In the last case, and possibly the fact may furnish a clue, the body was brought to the railway arch in some covering, which, with its bloodstains, was not left behind. It was reported that on Wednesday, under a plank close to St, Philip's church, Oxford-street, Stepney, now in course of erection, a police-constable found a portion of a woman's course apron, which was stained with something resembling coagulated blood a few days old. The police, however, profess entire ignorance of the discovery.

LATER:

The suggestion that the woman died of poison has been made, and the presences of bruises upon the arms has been mentioned as supporting the theory that there was a struggle shortly before death. The police have, they readily admit, a very difficult task before them, but they are not without hopes of ultimate success. Although, of course, the Home-office has been fully apprised of everything that has come to the ears of the Chief Commissioner since the body was found, no reward has yet been offered for the arrest of the criminal, and it is not deemed likely that such a course will be resorted to.

The police have carried out a careful examination of all places where they might possibly find the missing portions of the body, or the locality where the murder was perpetrated. Of course, without the head, identification is a matter of the utmost difficulty, as the body does not appear to have any distinguishing marks or peculiarities. Neither is much assistance afforded in this direction by the torn and blood-stained garment which partially enveloped the trunk. In most of the previous East-end murders the clothing has aided in the identification, and it will be recollected that the marking upon some of the clothing found with the Battersea remains enabled the police to trace the movements of the murdered woman up to within a comparatively short time previous to her death. The railway arch under which Tuesday's discovery was made is now completely boarded up.

The extraordinary possession which the Whitechapel mysteries have taken of the public mind may be gathered from the fact that the people are now beginning to see visions and dream dreams in which the murderer appears. That is probable enough, considering the excitement into which many people have been thrown. But when it comes to professing to see the murderer of one's dreams in an inoffensive gentleman sitting blamelessly at evening church, as one good lady professes to have done, one may well begin to fear lest some unlucky person may get arrested or lynched in consequence of these supernatural revelations.

Talking of dreaming about the Whitechapel murderer, how came it that Mr Stuart Cumberland, the most prominent of these dreamers, was permitted to go in and view the body of the latest victim? It is not stated that Mr Cumberland "represented" anything or anybody – except himself.

Superintendent Arnold and Inspector Reid were on Wednesday informed that on a wall on the corner of Frederick-street, which is a very dark passage in the rear of the spot where the trunk was found, some five or six words were chalked up, in which the name of "Joe Cleary" was introduced. In view of the statement published by a morning paper that it had been informed on Sunday, by a man giving the name of Cleary, that a murder had been committed, this was looked upon as a singular coincidence. Not very much importance, however, was attached to the matter, in consequence of the quantity and generally miscellaneous character of the chalk-writing on the wall, which obviously could in no way be connected with the crime. Several persons applied to the police for permission to view the remains, but only those who were able to show that more than the gratification of morbid curiosity would be gained were allowed to do so.

There was a painful scene at the conclusion of the inquest. The coroner had left when a most respectable-looking woman, careworn with grief, came into the room. She pointed to some police officers and exclaimed "That's my girl! Let me see her at the mortuary." The woman poured forth her tale in a half-sobbing way. She explained that her name was Smith, and the she lived in Jessamine-street, East-street, Old Kent-road. She left 66, Addington-road, West Croyden about three months ago, and, singular to say, she had lately noticed an advertisement, with an address given at a bookseller's office, alluding to her daughter. This, the mother thinks, was but a trap to catch her girl, who was suddenly missed from her home on Wednesday last, and no findings of her have since been ascertained. She was 17 years of age. As the deceased woman whose body was at St, George's mortuary was much older and had tapering fingers, it was pointed out that it could not be her daughter, The police offered to assist the poor woman in every way in their power to recover the lost girl. The mother, disconsolate and sobbing, expressed her thanks, and left the vestry building.

A number of theories respecting this supposed crime are being discussed. Some people are inclined to believe that the miscreant who threw Whitechapel into a state of terror last year, and is supposed to have resumed his operations in July, has determined to show that he can defy detection, and wishes to surpass in atrociousness anything which he has yet attempted. But it is admitted that if this version be correct, then the hitherto generally accepted theory that the Whitechapel murderer is a man possessed with some fearful form of uncontrollable mania falls to the ground, unless it is possible to assume that on occasion he could so bridle his passion that he might in cold blood, and at his leisure, proceed to the mutilation and dismemberment of his victims. It will also be recollected that the Whitehall and subsequent Thames mysteries were occupying the public mind at the same time as some of the former Whitechapel murders, and no connection between them was then traced. Tuesday's discovery bears a very close resemblance to the West End cases, the mode of procedure having been almost identical, while the strong point of difference is the change of locality. If the Chelsea dissector is still at work, and his motives were never made clear, he must, it is thought, have purposely removed his quarters to the East End, or have conveyed the body which he wished wo get rid of thither, with the intention of availing himself of the reputation of the undiscovered murderer, and to prevent a search being made for him in other parts of London. He may have taken this step, when he found that it was impossible, decomposition having set in, safely to dispose of the remains in any other way, but nevertheless he ran great risks of detection, for

Whitechapel, owing to the dock strike, has latterly been full of police by day and by night. One circumstance which is favourable to the detectives is that if the man came from the West End to the East he must have had a cart or a cab, as he could not have carried a bulky package in the dead of night without being noticed. It is considered that he had sufficient reasons for concealing the identity of the woman by removing the head; but, although the same precaution was adopted in the Battersea case, the police, mainly by means of the clothing, succeeded in proving that the woman had belonged to the lowest class, and was pretty well known. This matter appears to have led the author of the Pinchin-street mystery to destroy any clue which clothing could afford.

Dundee Evening Telegraph - Friday 20 September 1889

ALLEGED IDENTIFICATION OF "JACK THE RIPPER."

EXTRAORDINARY STATEMENT.

A curious story was published in the columns of the New York Herald (London edition) yesterday. It is to the effect that a man has been found who is quite convinced that the Whitechapel murderer occupied rooms in his house. When he left his lodgings a quantity of bows, feathers, and flowers, and other articles which belonged to the lower class of women, were found in his room.

The individual who supplies the above story has (according to the New York Herald) reason to believe that another murder will be committed shortly. Some writing to this effect, and said to be written by the suspected man, was found on a wall the other day. A sketch upon paper of a significant character has also been picked up near to the spot where the last victim's body was found. On Wednesday afternoon a reporter had an interview with Dr Forbes Winslow with reference to the above story, which, the Herald stated, had been communicated to Dr Winslow in the first instance.

"Here are Jack the Ripper's boots," said the doctor, at the same time taking a large pair of boots from under his table. Besides these noiseless coverings, the doctor says he has the "Ripper's" ordinary walking boots, which are very dirty, and the man's coat, which is also blood-stained. Proceeding, Dr Winslow said that on the morning of the 30th of August a woman, with whom he was in communication, was spoken to by a man in Worship Street, Finsbury. He asked her to come down a certain court with him, offering her £1. This she refused, and he then doubled the amount, which she also declined. She then watched him into a certain house, the situation of which the doctor would not describe. She previously noticed the man because of his strange manner, and on the morning of which the woman Mackenzie was murdered (July 17) she saw him washing his hands in the yard of the house referred to.

He was in his shirt sleeves at the time, and had a very peculiar look upon his face. This was about four o'clock in the morning. The doctor said he was now waiting for a certain telegram, which was the only obstacle to his effecting the man's arrest. The supposed assassin lived with a friend of Dr Forbes Winslow's, and this gentleman himself told the doctor that he had noticed the man's strange behaviour. He would at times sit down and write 50 or 60 sheets of manuscript about low women, for whom he professed to have a great hatred. Shortly before the body was found in Pinchin Street last week the man disappeared, leaving behind him the articles already mentioned, together with a packet of manuscript, which, the doctor said, was in was exactly the same handwriting as the Jack the Ripper letters which were sent to the police. He had stated previously that he was going abroad, but a very few days before the body was discovered (the 10th of September) he was seen in the neighbourhood of Pinchin Street. The doctor is certain that this man is the Whitechapel murderer, and says that two days at the utmost will see him in custody. He could give a reason for the head and legs of the last murdered woman being missing. The man, he thinks, cut the body up, and then commenced to burn it. He had consumed the head and legs when his fit of the terrible mania passed, and he was horrified to find what he had done.

"I know for a fact," said the doctor, "that this man is suffering from a violent form of religious mania which attacks him and passes off at intervals. I am certain that there is another man in it besides the one I am after, but my reasons for that I cannot state. The police will have nothing to do with the capture. I am making arrangements to station six men round the spot where I know my man is, and he will be trapped." The public had laughed at him (the doctor went on to say), but on the Tuesday before the last body was discovered he had received information that a murder would be committed in two or three days. In conclusion Dr Winslow remarked, "I am as certain that I have the murderer as I am of being here."

Illustrated Police News - Saturday 21 September 1889

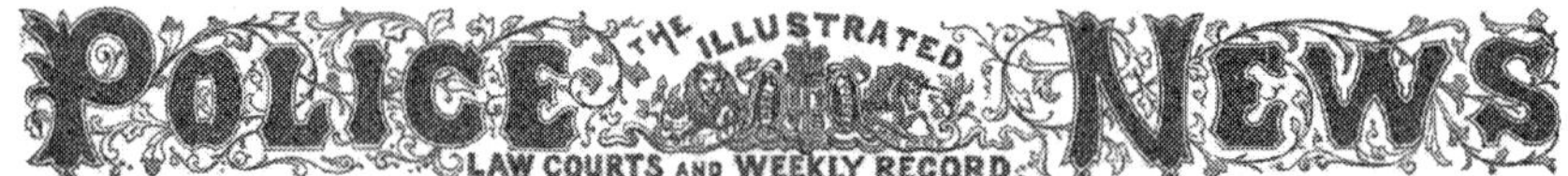

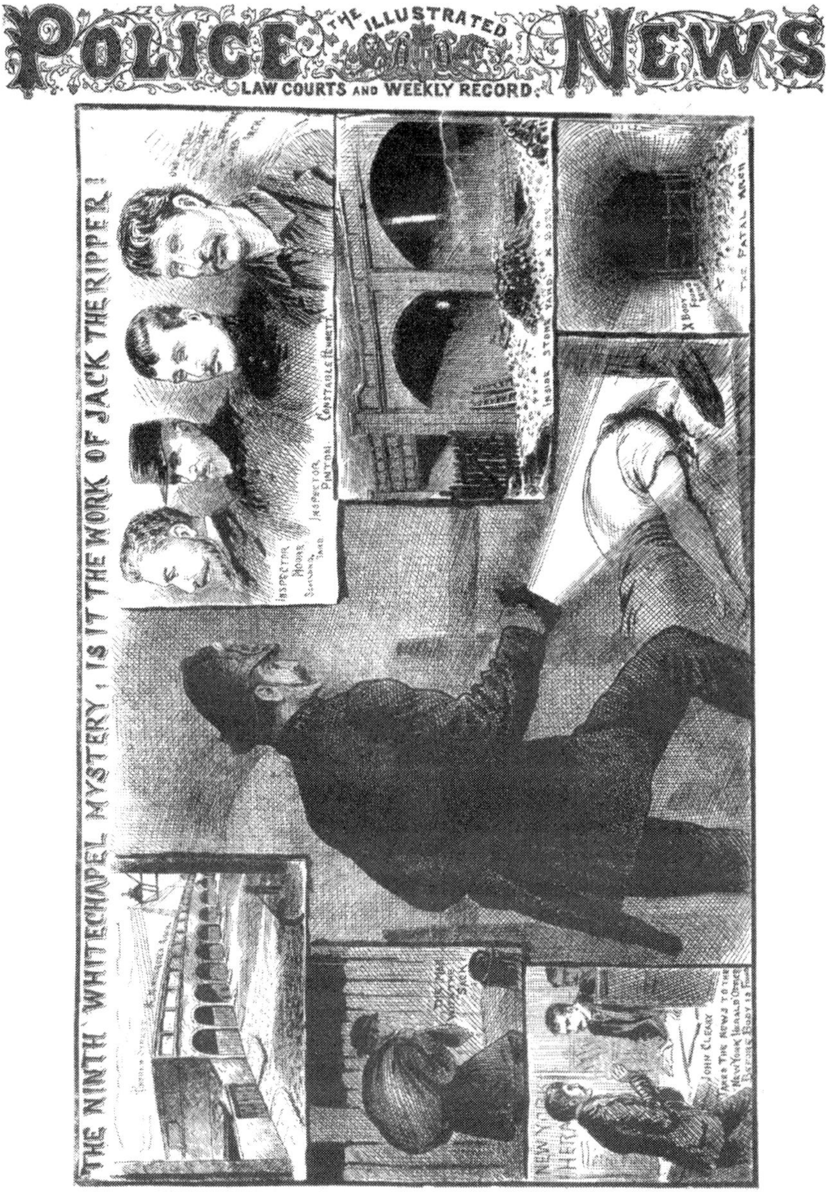
POLICE THE ILLUSTRATED NEWS
LAW COURTS AND WEEKLY RECORD.
THE NINTH WHITECHAPEL MYSTERY, IS IT THE WORK OF JACK THE RIPPER!

Portsmouth Evening News - Saturday 21 September 1889

THE LATEST CLUE.
WILL THE RIPPER BE CAUGHT?
DR. WINSLOW'S METHOD.

The Press Association says:- In the course of an interview, yesterday, Dr. Forbes Winslow said he wished in the first place to contradict the reports which credited him with the statement that he would be able, within three days, to put his hand upon the author of the Whitechapel atrocities. He thoroughly believed in the clue which he had obtained, but his evidence was circumstantial, and would take some time to piece together, and thoroughly work out. His informant was a respectable resident of Whitechapel, with whom the suspected "Jack the Ripper" lodged, and who had given him (Dr. Winslow) information which he regarded as valuable and practically conclusive. The doctor declined to state, very specifically, what this information was, but mentioned that a pair of noiseless boots and a bloody shirt were amongst the articles found in the suspected person's rooms. Again, the man had been seen loafing about the streets of Whitechapel late at night, and a woman with whom he (Dr. Winslow) was in communication had observed him washing his hands at a pump as early as four o'clock in the morning, shortly after the time which one of the murders was supposed to have been committed.

He (Dr. Winslow) had no desire to act as an amateur detective; he had plenty else to attend to in the way of his own profession, but he had taken this matter up because he believed the culprit to be a homicidal lunatic. He (the doctor) was, in fact, acting quite *pro bono publico*. One of the London evening papers had stated that it was his duty to inform the police of all he knew of the matter; his reply to this was that the police had been supplied with the same clue as now formed the basis of his own investigation, but they chose to ignore it. The landlord of the so-called "Jack the Ripper" was now in his (Dr. Winslow's) house, giving some further information. The suspected person, whose nationality was not known, for he spoke several languages equally well, left his lodgings some time ago, but had been seen in London as late as August 3rd last, and Dr. Winslow believes him to be in the metropolis now, though he could not give his address. There was some doubt as to whether he had ever belonged to the medical profession, but he was apparently a man in good circumstances. He had a mania respecting the women of the street, and have covered 50 or 60 pages with writing about them.

Dr. Winslow, who appeared thoroughly earnest and determined in manner, said of course his was but a theory after all, but felt thoroughly convinced that he was on the right track. Asked what method he proposed to adopt with view to bringing the culprit to justice, Dr. Winslow said that he intended to disguise himself shortly - he would not say what night - and proceed to Whitechapel, there to pursue his investigations in person. For obvious reasons he refrained from particularising the nature of his disguise, but intended it to be an effectual one. When in Whitechapel he would put himself in communication with the woman referred to, and also with half-a-dozen men who knew the suspected person. He hoped by this means to find him, and eventually prove him guilty of the crime. He did not believe, however, that "Jack the Ripper," if discovered, would be executed, as he was undoubtedly of unsound mind.

The Ripper's Accomplice

It may now be stated with safety, says a London contemporary, that there is every reason to believe that the East-end terror had an accomplice, and that his name was "Dodger." The man who is assumed to be "Jack the Ripper" was in the habit of receiving letters and postcards from a person who signed himself "Dodger." In this connection the whereabouts of John Cleary would be useful just now. Some of the parties in this movement are disposed to associate him with the "Dodger." Having read the description of the man who gave the information to the New York Herald on Sunday before the discovery in Pinchin-lane, they are inclined to think that he is the man who has been seen in the company of the alleged "Ripper." This may be only a coincidence; still, it is regarded as a remarkable one by many, and notably by a lady who yesterday took part in a conference on the subject of the murders. This lady, from the first murder to the present, has interested herself in the hue and cry, and made herself personally acquainted with the leading features of the crimes. She has acted as an amateur detective, and discovered many leading clues, which she has duly communicated to the police, only to be repulsed. Possessing a full knowledge of the clue upon which Dr. Forbes Winslow is working, and being a well known thought-reader, she is understood to distinctly affirm a connection between John Cleary and the "Dodger." She is convinced that once she sees the murderer she will be able to identify him. This lady has lent valuable aid in the investigation, and is as ardent a believer in the correctness of the clue as is the discoverer.

Description of the Supposed Murderer.

The other parties to the conference included the man who lodged the ubiquitous “Jack the Ripper.” He is a youngish man, tall, slightly-built, with a thin face and dark moustache. By trade he is a mechanical engineer. For some time past he has not been troubled with too much work, and, like a good citizen and a patriot, he has devoted his leisure time to searching for his lost lodger. He has now found regular employment, which starts on Monday, and so has handed the tracing of the notorious criminal to others. The “Ripper” lived with this gentleman about three months. The terror of the East End women is described as a gentlemanly kind of fellow. He was well educated, and well off, of a quiet but taciturn disposition, and irregular habits. He frequently went home in the small hours, and when questioned used to say that he had been out to post letters. He boasted of his surgical knowledge, and told wonderful stories of his medical experience. This gave rise to the belief that he had been a medical student. He used frequently to advise members of the family regarding their health, and knew more about their past ailments than they did themselves. He sometimes referred to America, and spoke of returning to that country shortly. It was not thought that he was an American, but from his knowledge of that country he had undoubtedly visited it. He was often seen prowling about shady quarters, inquiring where this court led to, and where that went, and talking with women of questionable character, treating them in public-houses, and accompanying them along the streets.

An Absurd Scare.

An unusually exciting incident took place last night in High-street, Kirkcaldy. A stranger to the town was seen walking in the vicinity of the West-end, when he was followed by a number of youths, who got up a cry that his long flowing beard was a false one, and that he was possibly the much-wanted "Jack the Ripper." Very shortly he became the object of intense curiosity, being followed by several hundreds people, and he was compelled to seek for safety. He hurried along the street, pursued by a yelling mob, now made up of young and old, who even went the length of pelting him with stones. Ultimately he took refuge in the police office, around the door of which his pursuers congregated and clamoured. After remaining some time in the office, where he had his tall hat exchanged and otherwise disguised himself, the police deemed it advisable to let the victim out by another door, when he made good his escape unobserved. He proved to be a commercial traveller on a visit to Kirkcaldy from the North.

Pall Mall Gazette - Tuesday 24 September 1889

THE WHITECHAPEL HORROR. RESUMPTION OF THE INQUEST.

The adjourned inquest on the body of a woman unknown, found under a railway arch in Pinchin-street, Whitechapel, was resumed this morning before Mr. Wynne E. Baxter, coroner for the South-Eastern Division of Middlesex, at the vestry-hall, Cable-street,

Superintendent Arnold and Detective-Inspector Moore and Inspector Reed represented the police.

Mr. Clarke, assistant to Dr. Phillips said a little before six o'clock on the morning of the 10th inst. he was called by the police to see the body of a woman, minus the head and legs, lying under a railway arch in Pinchin-street. The arms were not severed from the body. There was no pool of blood, or any signs of a struggle having taken place there. On moving the body he found there was a little blood underneath where the neck had bled. It was small in quantity and not clotted, and it had oozed from the wounds. There were the remnants of what had been a chemise over the body. The chemise had been torn down the front, and had been cut out from the front of the armhole on each side, these cuts appeared to have been made by a knife. The chemise was bloodstained, through being wrapped over the cuts on the neck. The body was removed on an ambulance to St. George's mortuary. On re examining it there he found the body appeared to be that of a woman of stoutish build, of dark complexion, about five feet three inches in height, and between thirty and forty years of age. He thought the body had been dead about twenty-four hours. Besides the wounds caused by the severance of the head and legs there was a wound fifteen inches long through the external coats of the abdomen. The body had not the appearance of having been recently washed. On the back were four bruises all caused before death. One of the bruises might have been caused by a fall or a kick. On the right arm there were eight distinct bruises, and seven on the left, all recent and caused before death. The back of both forearms and hands were much bruised. On the outer side of the left fore-arm, three inches above the wrist, was a cut about two inches in length, and lower down there was another cut. Both were caused before death. The bruises might have been caused by the right arm being tightly grasped. There was an old injury on the index finger of the right hand. The hands and nails were pallid, but were not indicative of any particular kind of work. There were no signs that the deceased had been a mother.

Dr. Phillips spoke to his examining the body, and he confirmed the evidence given by Dr. Clarke. The cut surfaces where the thighs had been removed were nearly dry, whilst the cut surface of the neck was not so dry. The skin was beginning to peel, and the decomposition of the body was greater above than below the lower part of the trunk. Dr. Phillips went on to say that in the presence of Dr. Gordon Brown and Mr. Hibbard he had further examined the body. The neck had been severed by a clean instrument, commencing a little to the right side behind. It had severed the whole of the structures of the neck, dividing the cartilage of the neck in front and separating the bones of the spine behind. The two small cuts mentioned on the arm appeared to him as likely to have been caused with the sweep of the knife when dividing the muscle covering the upper part of the thigh. The marks upon the fingers had fairly healed, and had evidently been in a process of healing for some time previous to death. He thought that the pallor of the hands and nails were important elements, enabling him to draw a conclusion as to the cause of death. The length of the trunk he found to be 2 ft. 3 in., whilst the length of forearm and hand were 16¼ in. He removed a small quantity of hair for the sake of future identification. The weight of the body was 67 lb. There was throughout the body an absence of blood from the vessels. The heart was empty. There was a slight collapse of the intestines, and the womb he believed to be unimpregnated. He believed the woman must have been under forty years of age.

In reply to a question of the coroner, Dr. Phillips said he believed that the mutilation of the body was subsequent to death, though the mutilation was effected by some one accustomed to cut up animals or seeing animals cut up; and that the incisions were effected by a strong knife, eight inches or more long. In reply to a juryman, he said that the fruit found in the stomach was stone fruit, such as plums. In reply to another question, he stated that he had no opinion as to whether the murderer possessed human anatomical skill, and added that men engaged in the cutting up of animals acquired great facility in separating the various parts of animals.

Michael Keeting, of No. 1, Osborne-street, Brick-lane, licensed shoe black, stated that he went to sleep in one of the railway arches in Pinchin street on the night preceding the discovery of the body. He went to sleep there because he did not have the price of a lodging. He got under the arch between eleven and twelve o'clock, but did not remember noticing anyone around the arch. He was aroused by the police, and on leaving saw something on the left side of the arch. He could not say whether the body was there when he went in to sleep as he was the worse for drink. He lent the police his sack as covering for the body. He had never slept in the archway before, nor had he known of it, but passing by it he considered it a quiet place in which to sleep,

Exeter Flying Post - Tuesday 24 September 1889

THE WHITECHAPEL MURDER.
RESUMED INQUEST.

This morning Mr. Wynne E. Baxter resumed the inquest at the Vestry Hall, Cable-street, concerning the death of the woman, unknown, whose trunk was discovered on the 10th inst. under the railway arch, in Pinchin-street, Whitechapel.

Richard Hawk, a sailor, of St. Ives, Cornwall, who also slept in this arch, said he went there at twenty minutes past four in the morning. He knew the time because he asked a policeman. (Laughter.) He saw nothing under the railway arch as he went in.

Jeremiah Hirley, living near Pinchin-street, said he was called by the police constable on the beat at 5 o'clock, on the day the discovery was made. He left home twenty-five minutes late and saw a man, apparently a Jew tailor, standing at the corner just near. This was the only person he saw about.

Dr. Phillips was recalled, and asked by the Coroner whether there was any similarity in the cutting up between the present case, and the murder in Dorset-street last November? The doctor asked to be allowed to postpone his answer.

Detective-Inspector Moore produced a number of plans of the locality, and stated that despite every effort the body had not been identified. He saw no reason for adjourning the inquiry. He produced a chemise found in the trunk, which apparently had been made by a somewhat unskilful needlewoman.

At this point Dr. Phillips said he would answer the coroner's question. He did not see any similarity in the cutting of the legs, but the division of the neck and the attempt to disarticulate the bones of the spine were very similar. The savagery shown in Dorset-street, however, far exceeded anything in the present case. In the former case the mutilations were most wanton, whereas, in this case, they appeared to have been made for the purpose of disposing of the body.

This concluded the evidence, the Coroner having remarked that he did not think any good purpose would be served by further adjourning the enquiry. The Coroner briefly summed up the case, commenting upon the remarkable fact that no one of a suspicious character had been seen in the neighbourhood anywhere near at the time when the trunk must have been deposited under the arch.

The jury returned a verdict of "Wilful murder" against some person or persons unknown.

Pall Mall Gazette - Thursday 26 September 1889

THE WHITECHAPEL MYSTERY.

It is stated that the police have discovered the whereabouts of the man John Cleary, who made some statements at the office of a newspaper in London immediately before the recent discovery of the mutilated body of a woman in Pinchin-street, Whitechapel. The police have satisfied themselves that the story told by Cleary - who, by the way, could not be found at the address which he gave at the time - was worthless. *The Times* says Cleary appears to be known to the police as a vendor of evening newspapers in the streets of London, but we hear that he really was engaged as porter in a newspaper office.

Shields Daily Gazette - Saturday 28 September 1889

THE PINCHIN STREET MURDER.

It is stated that the father and mother of the girl named Emily Barker, Northampton, feel convinced that she was the victim of the Pinchin Street Whitechapel murder. The girl had been rescued from a wild life by a London missionary, but escaped from him two days before the murder.

Gloucester Citizen - Monday 30 September 1889

THE WHITECHAPEL MURDER.

It is stated that the father and mother of the girl named Emily Barker, of Northampton, feel convinced that she was the victim of the Pinchin-street Whitechapel murder. The girl had been rescued from a wild life by a London missionary, but escaped from him two day's before the murder. The mother says she is satisfied as to the identity, and that she made the chemise which was found by the police. The mother also says her suspicions are confirmed by a mark on the finger. The

Northampton police are in communication with the London police respecting the matter.

During the past week several letters, purporting to be written by Jack the Ripper, have been found and handed over to the police. The last was, on Saturday evening, discovered in Victoria-road, Kensington, and was to the effect that the writer would do another murder, at the corner of Pinchin-street, Whitechapel, and the police who wore indiarubber shoes should be cautious.

Daily Gazette for Middlesbrough - Monday 30 September 1889

"JACK THE RIPPER'S" NEXT MURDER. ANOTHER LETTER.

On Saturday evening the Press Association received a letter, bearing the East London post mark, purporting to be from "Jack the Ripper." The envelope was apparently addressed by a different person to the writer of the letter, which was written on a torn single sheet of notepaper, and was as follows:-

"E, 28 September. Dear Editor,- I hope to resume operations about Tuesday or Wednesday night. Don't let the 'coppers' know. "Jack the Ripper."

The envelope was smeared with red ink, and the signature was underlined with red ink.

Another correspondent says that during the past week several letters purporting to have been written by "Jack the Ripper" have been found and handed over to the police authorities, besides chalk writing on walls, having reference to the same individual's intention to visit a certain locality on a certain night. The last letter handed to the police was on Saturday evening, this being found in Victoria-road, Kensington. It was to the effect that "Jack the Ripper" would do another murder at the corner of Pinchin street, Whitechapel, and it cautioned the police who were in india-rubber shoes.

THE SUPPOSED IDENTITY OF THE VICTiM.

There is reason to believe that the victim of the Pinchin-street murder was a Northampton girl named Emily Barker, who after a quarrel with her mother ran away from home. The father aud mother of the girl feel convinced that she was the Whitechapel murderer's latest victim. The girl had led a wild life, and the last heard of her was that she had been picked up on a London doorstep in a semi-nude state by a London Missionary. She escaped suddenly from his charge two days before the murder was discovered. The mother says she is satisfied as to the identity, and that she made the chemise which was found by the police. The mother also says her suspicions are confirmed by a mark on the finger. There is no doubt about the fact that the girl did find her way to Whitechapel, that she was friendless there, and that she endured some terrible privations after she left home. The garment found with the body had been washed and found to be made of Horrocks' calico, and that it is hand-sewn, and stitched in an inferior manner. The mother of the girl Emily Barker, it is alleged, says she made her daughter a similar garment, but whether it is the same has yet to be proved. The descriptions of the girl and the remains in many respects are believed to correspond, with the exception of the age; the body, according to medical opinion, being that of a somewhat older person. On this point, however, it is admitted there may be some room for doubt. It is alleged that the mother is positive, and if so a very searching enquiry will have to be institute, and a probable clue may be obtained.

Leeds Mercury - Tuesday 01 October 1889

THE LASTEST WHITECHAPEL MURDER.

The authorities at Scotland-yard, after careful investigation, have come to the conclusion that the body recently found in Pinchin-street, Whitechapel, could not possibly be that of the girl Emily Barker, of Northampton, who has been missing for the last three weeks. The father of the girl came up to London yesterday, and had a long interview with the detectives who have the case in hand; but Mr. Barker's description of his daughter by no means tallies with that of the murdered woman, and he has returned to Northampton satisfied that the deceased was a stranger to him. In the first place, there was an important discrepancy in the matter of height. According to Mr. Barker's statement, his daughter was about 5ft. 4 in., and while plump and well-nourished was distinctly petite in appearance. So far as can be gathered from the characteristics of the dismembered trunk, the murdered woman must have been a person of very different physique. Her height would be at least 5ft. 8in. or 5ft. 9in., her limbs above the average size, and her frame generally that of an almost abnormally developed female. But the most important feature in the case is the absence from the mutilated body of a peculiar mark known to exist on the body of Emily Barker. One of the first questions asked by Mr. Barker was in reference to this mark, but on turning up the official descriptions of the trunk, it was soon found that this important item in the identification was lacking.

There seems to be no doubt, however, that the girl Emily Barker did find her way to Whitechapel; that she was friendless there; and that she endured some terrible privations after she left home. The Rev. Mr. Winter, curate of St. John's Church, Bethnal Green, who had some knowledge of Miss Barker, says – It was about six o'clock on the first Friday evening in this month that I was told that a young girl wanted to see me. I asked her what she wanted, and she told me that she wanted to know if I could assist her back to Northampton. She wanted me to pay her fare, as she said she wanted to go back home to her father. I was very short with her, and told her I had no funds for any such purpose. She told me she came to London on the previous Monday, and as she did not know where to go she went and procured a night's lodging at the Salvation Army's shelter in Whitechapel. I have no Home for girls, and as so many are given to lying, I preferred not to have much to say to her; but I got one of my female helps to interview her. She said that on the first night she had to pay 3d. for her night's lodging at the Salvation Army; but when she went the second night she had no money, and they would not take her in. They told her that if she was a fallen girl, and if she would admit it, they would send her to one of their Homes. She, however, persistently refused to make such an admission. As she did not possess any money, she said that the next night she walked about Whitechapel, and at last got into Hanbury-street, where one of the murders was committed. She walked about in that dark street all one night. As I had no place to send her, I gave her the addresses of several places for girls. She, however, elected to go back to the Salvation Army, and I gave her 3d. I telegraphed to her father, and he replied that he could not have her back, as it would only cause another row in his house. She did not return to me on the following morning, and what became of her I do not know. In appearance she was rather short, dark, and plump.

Penny Illustrated Paper - Saturday 12 October 1889

The trunk of the unidentified woman discovered on the 12th ult., in a railway arch at Pinchin-street, Backchurch-lane, was buried last Saturday morning in Plaistow Cemetery.

Daily Gazette for Middlesbrough - Saturday 23 November 1889

THE LAST WHITECHAPEL MURDER. SUPPOSED IDENTIFICATION OF THE VICTIM.

Mrs Georgina Smith, a widow, of 6, Jesmond-street, Old Kent-road, made a statement yesterday morning with reference to the mysterious absence of her daughter, Rosina Lydia Smith, who was missed from her home shortly before the discovery of the trunk of a woman under a railway arch in Pinchin street, Whitechapel. Mrs Smith states that a man who resided near Redhill, a farmer and cattle dealer, met the girl (who was then accompanied by her brother) near the Monument. Having given them refreshment, the boy went with the man down to a place near Tunbridge Wells on the plea that the lad would be given some farm work. The youth returned to London (he alleged he had been assaulted), and the girl was afterwards missed, and has never since been seen alive. Mrs Smith adds that her daughter had an old injury on the index finger of her right hand (such an injury was on the hand of the deceased person found in Pinchin-street), and in other respects the description of the body, with the exception of the supposed age given by the medical men, resembles that of the girl Rosina Smith. Mrs Smith has expressed an intention of laying all the facts of the case before Mr Monro, the Chief Commissioner.

Dundee Courier - Tuesday 14 October 1890

THE "JACK RIPPER" SCARE. FURTHER REVELATIONS.

In connection with the extraordinary revelations published yesterday, a press representative has made further inquiries in Whitechapel, and has succeeded in ascertaining many important facts with regard to the suspicious circumstances related by Mr Backert. It appears that while the woman who told the strange story was living at the top floor of a block of model dwellings in the neighbourhood of Aldgate, the man engaged, on the floor below, a bedroom with lumber room adjoining, and paid her to keep the former clean, her occupation being that of an office cleaner. The lumber room, which contained a sink, was always kept locked, and, although she did a portion of her tenant's washing, it was evident he did much of it himself. She describes him as young, of middle height, well built, with a small fair moustache, and light brown hair, although she had frequently remarked that he had means by which he made his moustache and eyebrows much darker on some occasions than others. On one occasion he gave the woman a dark coloured overcoat to sell, and she offered it to the wife of a working man. The latter, however, pointed out that it was so stained with blood that she would not let her husband wear it. The patches, which were of a dull brown, were thought by the woman to be paint, but when she returned it to the mysterious lodger with an intimation that she could not sell it because of the blood, he laughed lightly, saying the stains were nothing. Nevertheless, he burnt the coat, for she subsequently discovered the remains, together with the horn buttons, in the grate. As the murders were committed her suspicions were increased, but she did not communicate them to any one until the day following the discovery of the body in Pinchin Street. She went to the bedroom as usual, when she found upon the three mats foot marks of blood, and upon one a large clot of the same substance. She then spoke of her suspicions to an official connected with the model buildings, but he, evidently believing that an arrest would bring the buildings into disrepute, advised her to say nothing of the matter. As time went on, and the murders continued, she saw in his room many articles which were blood stained, although he never would allow her to enter the room alone, but remained with her while she performed her work. With regard to the "Jack the Ripper" post cards, the man always wrote his letters in red ink, of which he had a large bottle on the mantel shelf. On the night of each of the murders he was absent, and returned at early morning. On the morning of the Castle Alley-murder he disappeared, having previously sold the whole of his belongings. The woman afterwards removed, but few days ago she again saw him near Aldgate, and this fact, combined with the letters recently published in the press, led her to lay the facts before Backert. She also states that the man has recently married.

ANOTHER THREAT.

Yesterday morning a knife and a letter signed "Jack the Ripper" were found in Love Lane, Wandsworth. The writer stated that he was once more to "commence operations."

Also Available

LOCH NESS:
From Out Of The Depths
Original Newspaper Accounts of the Rise of the Loch Ness Monster, 1933-1934

In 1933 “Nessie” erupted into the public consciousness with a deluge of sightings of “something” in the waters of the 22 mile long and 700 foot deep Scottish loch. Since then the Loch Ness Monster has captured the public imagination more than any other cryptid creature.

Gathered in this book are the original newspaper accounts from the years 1933 and 1934, when “Nessie Fever” was at its height. Not just sightings, but plans for monster hunts and government responses to the appearance of this unknown creature are presented here.

Whatever your stance on the existence of the Loch Ness Monster, these accounts provide a fascinating insight into the happenings and opinions that swirled around Loch Ness in the early part of the 20th Century.

Available in paperback and for Kindle from Amazon.com

Also Available

The Guyra Ghost

Original Newspaper Accounts of Australia's Most Prominent Poltergeist Case

APRIL, 1921 – GUYRA, NSW. For over a month in 1921, the tiny town of Guyra in northern NSW was the focus of national attention as events unfolded that would form the basis of Australia's most prominent poltergeist case, as the home of the Bowen family was bombarded by stones from nowhere, and the walls were pounded on by unseen hands.

Here, for the first time, is a collection of all the available newspaper articles that were published regarding the incident at the time. From this evidence you may draw your own conclusions. Hoax? Or a true case of paranormal phenomena...?

Available in paperback and for Kindle from Amazon.com

22283979R00184

Printed in Great Britain
by Amazon